DNA
FINGER-
PRINTING

DNA FINGER- PRINTING

CHRISTOPHER LAMPTON

An Impact Book

Franklin Watts
New York/London/Toronto/Sydney
1991

On the cover (clockwise from top left): computer graphic of DNA double helix; Alec Jeffreys, who first developed the DNA fingerprinting technique; results of a DNA fingerprint test—which suspect is culpable?

Photographs copyright © : The Bettmann Archive: p. 12; Stock Boston, Inc.: p. 29 (Spencer Grant); Cellmark Diagnostics/ICI Americas Inc.: p. 34; Lifecodes Corporation: p. 42; Professor Alec J. Jeffreys, FRS, University of Leicester: p. 46, 58; Kjell B. Sandved: p. 92; AP/Wide World Photos: p. 94.

Library of Congress Cataloging-in-Publication Data

Lampton, Christopher.
    DNA fingerprinting / by Christopher Lampton.
        p.   cm. — (An Impact book)
    Includes bibliographical references (p.   ) and index.
    Summary: Examines the procedures and uses of DNA fingerprinting as a method of identification in forensic science.
    ISBN 0-531-13003-7
    1. DNA fingerprints.   [1. DNA fingerprints.   2. Forensic sciences.]   I. Title.
    RA1057.55.L36   1991
    614'.1—dc20   91-16533 CIP AC

CONTENTS

DNA FINGER-PRINTING

ONE
FORENSIC SCIENCE

Detectives throughout history have sought the perfect method of catching criminals. And criminals have sought the perfect method of eluding detectives.

You would think that, in such an ongoing war, the detective would have all the advantages. After all, the detective has all of the resources of society on his or her side: technology, manpower (and womanpower), the cooperation of honest citizens. But the criminal has the advantage of stealth. By committing crimes in the dead of night or in secret places, the criminal seeks to erase all signs and clues that might inform the detective of his or her identity. A carefully planned crime can be a difficult thing to solve, no matter how many resources society places at the detective's disposal.

Fortunately, most crimes aren't very carefully planned. Criminals, on the whole, aren't as intelligent as detectives and they tend to act spontaneously, impulsively. They leave behind clues that the detective can use to trace their identities. And the clever detective pounces on those clues with a vengeance.

But clues aren't necessarily easy to interpret. If the detective is lucky, there will be witnesses to the crime, witnesses who know the criminal's name and address and can give the detective directions on how to get there. If not, the detective will have to rely on indirect clues, and for the interpretation of those clues, the detective may need to turn to science.

The science of interpreting clues to a crime is called *forensics*. There are many branches of forensics. Forensic pathology, for instance, is the study of dead bodies to determine how they died. If the crime being investigated is murder, the forensic pathologist can tell the detective how and when the murder occurred. If the cause of death is still obscure, a forensic toxicologist can analyze the body for signs of poisoning. Forensic anthropologists analyze the bones of the victim to help determine just who the hapless person was, and forensic odontologists study the victim's teeth for much the same purpose.

A forensic psychologist can look at the crime as a whole and make an educated guess about the kind of person who might have committed it, giving the detective important clues toward finding that person. Furthermore, the forensic psychologist can study the criminal once he or she has been captured, to determine if the individual is mentally sound enough to stand trial.

The study of the physical evidence—the clues— left at the scene of a crime is called *criminalistics.* Forensic chemists and biologists analyze everything from hairs found on the victim's clothing to chips of paint lodged under the heel of the victim's shoes. Perhaps the best-known branch of criminalistics is *fingerprinting,* which studies the distinctive markings often left behind when an object is touched by someone's bare fingertips.

Look closely at the tips of your fingers. Tiny lines of flesh, called the *papillary ridges,* lace their way across the skin of your fingertips in distinctive, often surprisingly attractive, patterns. These are your fingerprints. Because the fingers secrete oils, these patterns can be transferred to any smooth surface that you touch. As you've probably been told, no two people have precisely the same fingerprints. This makes fingerprinting a powerful tool for identifying the presence of a suspect at the scene of a crime. If the suspect's fingerprints are there, then the suspect must have been there, too (though not necessarily at the time the crime was being committed).

The science of fingerprinting is only a little more than a century old. In 1880, the magazine *Nature* published a letter from Dr. Henry Faulds, who worked at a hospital in Tokyo. Not only did fingerprints come in a wide variety, Faulds noted in this letter, but they never changed; at seventy, a person still had the same fingerprints they had been born with. Thus, fingerprints would make an ideal method of identifying criminals. In fact, another correspondent to the same magazine later noted that he had been using exactly this technique to keep track of prisoners and government pensioners in Bengal, India.

To make fingerprinting effective as a crime-fighting technique, it was necessary for someone to make an organized study of fingerprint patterns and to collect the fingerprints of criminals in a systematic fashion. This work was begun in the 1890s by Sir Francis Galton, an early British researcher into the science of heredity, who convinced Scotland Yard (then, as today, the central British crime-fighting or-

ganization) to adopt fingerprinting as a major forensic technique.

Sir Richard Henry of Scotland Yard became an enthusiastic champion of fingerprinting technology. At Galton's urging, he began studying the technique in detail and by 1901 was ready to use it in practice, in solving crimes throughout the United Kingdom. Sir Richard's major contribution to forensics was in establishing a system for organizing fingerprints so that a fingerprint found at the scene of a crime could easily and quickly be compared with large numbers of fingerprints taken from known criminals.

This system, known as the Henry system, organizes fingerprints into eight different types, based on the central portion (or *pattern area)* of the print. The eight types are the plain arch, the tented arch, the radial loop, the ulnar loop, the plain whorl, the central pocket loop, the double loop, and the accidental. Because different fingers, even on the same hand, can have different patterns, the Henry system uses the prints from all ten fingers as the basis of classification. The fingerprint records are organized in large files according to pattern.

The Henry system quickly caught on across the Atlantic Ocean in the United States, where Leavenworth penitentiary in Kansas began fingerprinting federal prisoners in 1904. Soon thereafter, the Bureau of Criminal Identification of the International

Sir Francis Galton (1822–1911), English scientist. He published treatises on many subjects ranging from meteorology to heredity, but perhaps is best known for devising a system for fingerprint identification.

Association of Chiefs of Police began keeping its own files of fingerprints. In 1924, these two fingerprint collections were merged under the auspices of a single organization: the Federal Bureau of Investigation, better known as the FBI. Today, the FBI's collection of fingerprints numbers in the hundreds of millions.

From the detective's point of view, the ideal crime scene would contain a complete and perfect set of the perpetrator's fingerprints (and nobody else's), preferably on some object clearly used in the commission of the crime: the murder weapon, for instance, or a crowbar used to jimmy open a window in a burglary. This ideal scenario doesn't often happen, however. More often, the fingerprints recovered from the crime scene are smudged and incomplete. Only some fingers of the suspect's hands are represented, and those fingers are only represented partially. Even under these circumstances, fingerprints can be a useful tool—an expert can reconstruct the print of a finger from a partial impression. The FBI keeps files of individual prints in addition to its files of ten-finger prints, so even the print of a single finger can be used to narrow the field of suspects.

But sometimes criminals leave no fingerprints at all. Or they leave fingerprints so hopelessly smudged that even the most experienced expert cannot reconstruct them. And often even a perfect set of fingerprints is useless for proving guilt. If the crime occurred in the suspect's house, for instance—or even in a house that the suspect was known to have visited for perfectly innocent reasons—the presence of the suspect's fingerprints doesn't prove that he or she committed the crime, or even was present when it happened.

So, although fingerprints can be used to identify an individual uniquely, they are not the ideal forensic clue. What the detective needs, in addition to fingerprint evidence, is some sort of clue that not only uniquely identifies a person who was present at the scene of a crime, but that ties the person to the crime itself. And such a clue should ideally be useful even in relatively small quantities, or if smudged.

Blood has the potential for being such a clue. So does semen. Often the perpetrator of a crime is injured while the crime is being committed and leaves a quantity of blood behind. If the crime is rape, the perpetrator commonly leaves a sample of his semen on the victim. If this blood or semen could somehow be traced to a specific individual, it would represent a powerful, almost incontrovertible, proof that that individual was responsible for the crime.

Traditionally, both blood and semen have been identified forensically through *blood-typing*. A person's blood type depends on the presence of certain molecular structures on that person's blood cells. (You'll read more about cells and molecules in the next chapter.) These structures are known as *antigens,* and the two most common are known simply as A and B. A person whose blood cells bear the A antigens is said to have type A blood. A person whose blood cells bear the B antigens is said to have type B blood. A person whose blood cells have both A and B antigens is said to have type AB blood and a person whose blood cells have neither A nor B antigens has type O. Another chemical property, called the Rh factor, determines whether the person's blood is Rh negative or Rh positive.

Blood types are an important consideration in blood transfusions. Individuals with certain blood types can only be transfused with blood of that type or a compatible type. Thus, simple chemical tests are available that can determine blood type from a small sample of blood. And these tests can be used to determine the type of a sample of blood (or semen) found at the scene of a crime.

But, unless the perpetrator has an extremely rare blood type, these blood tests can only narrow the identification down to a percentage of the population—say 30 percent or 10 percent—rather than to a specific individual. Blood tests can suggest that a person *might* have committed a crime—and, on occasion, they can prove that a person certainly did *not* commit a crime. But they can rarely prove that a person indisputably *did* commit a crime.

From the detective's point of view, it would be much better if there were some way to take a blood or sperm sample (or a single hair or a piece of skin) found at the scene of a crime and show that that sample could have come from only one person out of the entire population of the planet Earth. If that were possible, then much of the uncertainty would be taken out of detective work. Criminals could be absolutely identified and their guilt could be unquestionably proven in court.

Until recently, there was no way to do this. But as biological technology has advanced inexorably in the late years of the twentieth century, so has forensic biological technology. A new technique known variously as DNA fingerprinting, genetic fingerprinting, and forensic DNA profiling has shown great promise as a method of identification. If this promise is realized—and some judges and lawyers believe that it already has been—then it may be possible to prove the guilt of certain criminals beyond the shadow of a doubt. There are other experts, however, who believe that the DNA fingerprinting technique may already have been overused and may not be as accurate as some forensic scientists believe.

How does DNA fingerprinting work? To understand the technique, we'll first have to look at the inner workings of the human cell, at the tiny structures called *chromosomes* that contain the working blueprint for the human body and all of the other molecules that make it function.

TWO
THE MOLECULAR I.D.

The human body is a marvelously complex thing. It is made up of an almost uncountable number of parts, all of which work together in intricate coordination. No machine shop has ever turned out a device as complex as a human body; no artist ever rendered a picture with such an order of detail.

No two human bodies are alike, except perhaps the bodies of identical twins. (And identical twins are different in tiny and surprising ways, since even twins aren't subject to exactly the same environment throughout their lives.) When you meet a friend, you don't need to examine their fingerprints to know who it is. You recognize the person by the shape of the eyes, the size of the nose, the color of the hair, the cadence of the voice. All of these differing features blend together to form an impression of uniqueness that belongs to that single individual and no other individual anywhere on the planet.

And yet the biological processes that create a human being from the combination of the mother's ovum and the father's sperm are identical for every human being. The cells that make up a fetus always divide in the same way and the metabolism of every individual functions in more or less the same manner. Where, then, do the variations between individuals come from? What makes each individual unique?

Part of this uniqueness comes from the environment in which the person grows up, which explains why even identical twins are never perfectly identical. But a large portion of the uniqueness is built in, inherent in the individual from the moment of conception. This uniqueness comes from the *genes*.

Although every individual may be unique, there are nonetheless resemblances between individuals, particularly when those individuals are from the same family. We laugh with delight when a baby turns out to have its mother's nose and its father's hair color, but we are not in the least bit surprised. We say that the child has inherited these features from the parents, but what the child has really inherited is the parents' *genes*.

What are genes? Originally, genes were nothing more than a concept, a means of explaining the way in which physical features were passed down from generation to generation. The first scientist to study genes was the Augustinian monk Gregor Mendel, who examined the inheritance of characteristics in pea plants in a monastery at Brunn, Austria, in the 1860s. Mendel noted that characteristics such as the color of the blossoms and the texture of the peas were passed down from generation to generation in well-defined ratios, almost as though some sort of "unit" (as Mendel called it) were being passed from parent to offspring in a random reshuffling.

In the twentieth century, scientists discovered that these units (which they had renamed genes) resided in structures called *chromosomes* which are found at the center of the living cell.

All living things are made of cells. You, the person holding this book, are made of literally trillions of cells, but don't bother looking for them. You'd need a fairly powerful microscope. Most cells are far too small to see with the naked eye.

The cells are where most of the real action in your body takes place. Each cell is filled with a kind of machinery that is working away even as you sit placidly in your chair, reading this book. This cellular machinery is engaged in the difficult but worthwhile job of keeping you alive. Without this cellular machinery, your heart would not beat, your lungs would not inhale and exhale, your mind would not think. You would be dead.

The machinery of the cell is made up of *molecules.* What is a molecule? It is a chain of *atoms,* the basic building blocks of all matter in the universe. The molecules found inside a cell, however, are unusually large, at least by the standards of molecules found in nonliving objects. And they are not simple, linear chains of atoms but twisted and knotted and folded chains that form complex structures.

Most of the molecules in your cells are of a special type called *protein* molecules. Protein molecules are large molecules made of a number of smaller molecules, called *amino acids,* linked together in a chain. There are twenty different kinds of amino acids used to build the protein molecules found in the human body, as listed in Table 1. The specific order in which these molecules occur in a protein molecule determines the shape of the molecule, and it is the shape of the molecule that determines the task for which the molecule is suited within the cell.

Perhaps the most important protein molecules found within a living cell are the *enzymes.* It is the

TABLE 1
THE AMINO ACIDS

Alanine	Threonine
Isoleucine	Tryptophan
Hydroxyproline	Valine
Methionine	Histidine
Tyrosine	Arginine
Leucine	Asparagine
Lysine	Serine
Cystine	Glutamine
Cysteine	Proline
Phenylalanine	Glycine

job of enzymes to promote chemical reactions between other molecules—that is, to take those molecules apart and put them back together again in new
ways. On the surface of each enzyme molecule are
found a number of indentations, called *active sites,*
where other molecules can be fitted into place long
enough for a chemical reaction to occur. The shape
of the active site determines what kind of chemical
reactions can take place there. When a chemical reaction is needed within the cell—and it is these
chemical reactions that keep the cell alive—an enzyme is created to make it happen.

How does the cell create enzymes? This is where
the molecules called chromosomes come into play.
The chromosomes are found at the center of the cell;
in higher organisms such as human beings, they are
found within a special compartment called the *nucleus.* Even by the standards of the cell, the chromosomes are large molecules. They have to be large.
The chromosomes are a library, a library that contains all of the information necessary for building
and running the organism of which the cell contain-

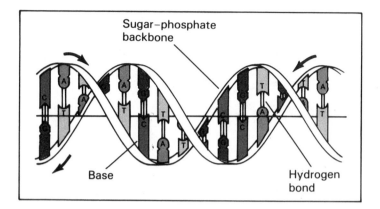

Figure 1. The DNA double helix is composed of four different nucleotide bases: adenosine (A), guanine (G), thymine (T) and cytosine (C). Adenosine pairs specifically with thymine, and guanine pairs specifically with cytosine.

ing the chromosome is a part. The chromosomes, in other words, are "made of" genes.

Unlike enzymes and other protein molecules, the chromosomes are not made of amino acids. Instead, they are made of deoxyribonucleic acid, DNA. The parts of DNA molecules that link together to form the large chromosomes are called nucleotides and they come in four varieties (or bases): adenosine, guanine, thymine, and cytosine, usually abbreviated as A, G, T, and C (Figure 1). These bases are the letters of the DNA alphabet. The information in the chromosome "library" is written in pairs of this alphabet, using a language called the genetic code.

What sort of information does the chromosome library contain? You might think of it as a kind of recipe book. Instead of recipes for cakes and cookies and chicken cacciatore, though, this recipe book contains recipes for making enzymes. Every enzyme

TABLE 2
The Genetic Code: Specific base
sequences code
for specific amino acids

Nucleotides	Amino Acids
UUU	phenylalanine
UUC	phenylalanine
UUA	leucine
UUG	leucine
UCU	serine
UCC	serine
UCA	serine
UCG	serine
UAU	tyrosine
UAC	tyrosine
UAA	stop
UAG	stop
UGU	cysteine
UGC	cysteine
UGA	stop
UGG	tryptophan
CUU	leucine
CUC	leucine
CUA	leucine
CUG	leucine
CCU	proline
CCC	proline
CCA	proline
CCG	proline
CAU	histidine
CAC	histidine
CAA	glutamine
CAG	glutamine
CGU	arginine

CGC	arginine
CGA	arginine
CGG	arginine
AUU	isoleucine
AUC	isoleucine
AUA	isoleucine
AUG	methionine
ACU	threonine
ACC	threonine
ACA	threonine
ACG	threonine
AAU	asparagine
AAC	asparagine
AAA	lysine
AAG	lysine
AGU	serine
AGC	serine
AGA	arginine
AGG	arginine
GUU	valine
GUC	valine
GUA	valine
GUG	valine
GCU	alanine
GCC	alanine
GCA	alanine
GCG	alanine
GAU	aspartic acid
GAC	aspartic acid
GAA	glutamic acid
GAG	glutamic acid
GGU	glycine
GGC	glycine
GGA	glycine
GGG	glycine

is a chain of amino acids linked together in a specific order. A chromosome recipe, therefore, is simply a list of amino acids in the order that they must be chained together to build that enzyme, written in the DNA alphabet according to the genetic code. Table 2 shows the words of the genetic code, where each "word" is a "three-letter" sequence of bases representing the name of an amino acid.

A genetic recipe for the sequence of amino acids cysteine-glutamine-tryptophan-arginine, for instance, might read TGCCTTTGGCGT, where every three bases form a single "word" of the genetic code. Of course, a complete genetic recipe would be hundreds of times longer than this.

When scientists speak of a "gene" today, they are referring to the recipe for a single protein spelled out on a chromosome in this genetic language. There are twenty-three chromosomes in every cell of the human body. Together they contain more than 100,000 of these recipes—that is, more than 100,000 genes.

Actually, there are twenty-three *pairs* of chromosomes in the human body, but the chromosome recipes in one half of each pair more or less duplicate the chromosome recipes in the other half. (Nonetheless, there can be differences between the two chromosomes in the pair.) One half of each pair (23 chromosomes) is inherited by an individual from his or her mother, the other half from his or her father, making for a total of 46 chromosomes. Since the parents *also* had twenty-three pairs of chromosomes, this means that one-half of the father's genes and one-half of the mother's genes are passed on. Which genes are inherited from which parent is determined more or less at random, which is why a son may have his mother's nose while his sister may have her father's nose. It's also possible for a quiet, or *recessive,* gene to be passed on from a parent to a child for a feature that neither parent exhibited, such as red hair (where both parents had dark hair) or blue eyes (where both parents had brown eyes). All of these features are determined by the specific enzyme recipes passed on in the chromosomes from parent to child.

When a cell needs to manufacture a specific protein molecule based on an enzyme recipe on a chromosome, it first uses enzymes to expose the bases along the portion of the chromosome containing the gene and other enzymes to copy the recipe from the chromosome to a molecule of RNA (short for ribonucleic acid, a "manufacturing" molecule related to DNA that carries out orders inscribed in DNA). The RNA copy of the recipe is then shuttled to the outer portions of the cell, where special molecular machinery "reads" the recipe and assembles the protein molecule that it describes.

As the human body (or any other organism) grows and evolves, it is sometimes necessary for it to create new cells. At this point, old cells divide in two, creating new cells through *fission,* or splitting. Each of the new cells must have a complete copy of the DNA library, so it's necessary for the chromosomes to copy themselves. They do this through a fascinating and elegant process called *DNA replication.* We don't need to go into the details of that process here —if you're interested, you might want to read a book on molecular biology to learn more. For our purpose it is enough to say that, with the aid of certain enzymes, the DNA molecules that we call the chromosomes are quite capable of making copies of themselves.

Every individual is unique because he or she is the product of a unique combination of genes passed down from both parents. Assuming that there are 100,000 genes in the human body and that you have an equal probability of inheriting either copy of the gene possessed by each parent, then there are

100,000 times 100,000, or 10 billion, possible sets of genes that you could have inherited from your parents.

However, this assumes that your parents had two *different* recipes, if you will, for every possible gene. In cases where your parents had *identical* genes for a particular characteristic, it really didn't matter which genes you got from which parent. A gene for brown eyes is still a gene for brown eyes, whether you got it from your father or your mother or both. Furthermore, most characteristics for which people carry genes don't vary as much as eye color or hair color does. All genes governing the functioning of a kidney, for instance, are probably pretty much alike. In fact, the great majority of the genes handed down from parent to child are pretty much alike, with little variation between individuals. The truth is, the differences between individuals are based on a rather small percentage of their genes.

And yet even this small difference between individuals is enough to make every person on this planet unique. The chance that two people will ever be born with the same combination of genes (unless they are identical twins, who through a kind of genetic accident actually *do* receive identical combinations of genes) is virtually nil. We are all one of a kind, and the basis for our uniqueness lies in our genes.

Our genes, therefore, represent a kind of molecular ID. More than our fingerprints, more than our blood types, more than any other thing about us (ex-

Every human being (identical twins excepted) has a unique set of genes. This accounts for our marvelous diversity as a species.

cept our personalities, which exist at least in part independently of our genes), the genes uniquely identify us. If it were possible to take a single cell anonymously from some individual and read the sequence of genetic recipes in that cell, we could unfailingly identify the individual from whom the cell was taken.

The application to forensic science is obvious. The forensic scientist looks for ways to identify individuals present at the scene of a crime through analysis of evidence left at that scene. And the best pieces of evidence are those that actually come from the perpetrator's body itself—blood, skin cells, semen, hair—because those pieces are unlikely to have been left behind by someone not involved in the crime.

Blood, skin cells, semen, hair—these things have something very special in common. They all contain cells from the body of the person they once belonged to, and these cells have within them the genetic sequence that makes that person unique. If we could open up a skin cell or blood cell and accurately read the genetic sequence inside, then compare it to the genetic sequences of people who might have been present at the scene of a crime, we would have the perfect "fingerprint"—a genetic fingerprint that would point unequivocally to a single individual and prove inarguably (or nearly so) that they were involved in committing it.

Is this possible? Is there any way in which we can read—and compare—human genes?

Only twenty years ago, the answer would have been a resounding no. Although scientists have understood the nature of the genes since the 1950s, their ability to "read" the genes has been largely indirect. And even when the genes can be read, the processes by which they are read are so slow and expensive as to be impractical for any forensic applications.

But over the past two decades that situation has changed. The methods by which scientists examine and manipulate genes have become steadily more sophisticated and precise.

One of the greatest breakthroughs in this emerging genetic technology was the invention of *recombinant DNA* in the early 1970s. This body of techniques involves the use of a special kind of protein molecule called a *restriction enzyme* to slice apart a DNA molecule so that parts of it can be extracted and inserted inside the genes of a completely different type of cell, such as a bacterium, where it can be studied in isolation.

What is a restriction enzyme? It is a kind of protein molecule manufactured by normal human cells (and the cells of other organisms as well) to fight off attacks by viruses. A virus is a semiliving organism that attaches itself to a cell and "injects" its own genes through the cell wall, effectively hijacking the protein manufacturing machinery of the cell, forcing it to turn out new copies of the virus (a process that ultimately destroys the cell). The cell fights back by creating restriction enzymes, which are rather like tiny molecular scissors that cut the viral genes into ribbons before they can cause damage to the cell.

In the early 1970s, scientists noticed that these restriction enzymes were often highly specific in the way that they sliced into the viral genes. Many of them would only cut the DNA molecules at a specific sequence of bases, such as CTGCAG. It occurred to a few scientists that restriction enzymes were more than just a weapon to be used by cells for fighting off viruses. They were also a tool that could be used by scientists for performing delicate surgery on chromosomes.

Suppose, for instance, you were a scientist who was interested in examining a specific gene on a specific chromosome. Through careful study, you have learned that the sequence of bases CTGCAG occurs on both sides of this gene. You could use the restriction enzyme that cuts this particular sequence of bases to slice this gene right out of the chromosome. (This particular restriction enzyme, by the way, is known to scientists as Pst 1.) You could then use other techniques (some of which we will examine in the next chapter) to separate the chromosome fragments containing this gene from other chromosome fragments, then place this gene inside a bacterium to study it.

How do restriction enzymes relate to forensic science? Well, there is as yet no easy method for determining the precise sequence of bases on the complete set of chromosomes taken from a human cell. (In fact, the United States government—in collaboration with the governments of several other countries—is currently engaged in trying to find such a method. This project, called the Genome Project, is being conducted under the leadership of James D. Watson. It will cost billions of dollars and is expected to take at least ten years. Obviously, it wouldn't be feasible to pay this kind of money or take this kind of time to solve a crime.) Thus, it is *not* yet feasible to compare the complete sequence of bases on a piece of DNA found at the scene of a crime with the complete sequence of bases on DNA taken from a crime suspect. But restriction enzymes can be used to create shortcut methods of analyzing the contents of a chromosome that can still be used to distinguish the chromosomes of one human being from another.

And it is these methods that lie behind the new forensic science of DNA fingerprinting.

THREE
GETTING THE
FINGERPRINT

In 1984, Alec Jeffreys, a geneticist (a scientist who studies genes) at the University of Leicester in England, was studying the evolution of genes. He had become interested in a genetic peculiarity known as the *intron.*

Not every base in a chromosome is part of a gene. Some sequences of bases are "nonsense" sequences, with no obvious meaning. They are not genetic recipes but more like marginal scribblings, parts of the genetic library that aren't really meant to be read.

These meaningless sequences are referred to as introns. (The more meaningful sequences of bases that make up the genes are sometimes known as *exons.)* Introns can occur at any point on a chromosome, even right in the middle of a gene. When the genetic recipes are copied to RNA molecules prior to being converted into proteins, the intron sequences are snipped out by special "editor" enzymes.

Why do introns exist at all? Some scientists believe that they are an important part of the evolu-

tionary process. Over thousands of years, the genes of a living organism can actually change, which is why organisms themselves change over time. Human beings today are very different from our human ancestors of 100,000 years ago because our genes are different, having been changed through the evolutionary force known as natural selection.

It is possible that introns represent genes that were useful long ago, in our distant ancestors, but that are no longer needed. Some kind of molecular switch has been turned on or off, removing these introns from the functioning portion of the genes, so that they are no longer used. In the distant future, however, they may be turned back on, becoming part of the genes once more in our distant descendants.

Jeffreys noticed an odd characteristic of introns. They are often made up of the same sequence of bases repeated over and over again. But the number of repetitions varies from individual to individual. In one person, a particular sequence of bases may be repeated five times, for example, while in another person it may be repeated fifty times. Why this should be the case, Jeffreys did not know. Yet it was obviously so. And it occurred to him that this might be a useful way of distinguishing one person's genes from another. The method by which he would do this hinged on the fact that molecules can be manipulated electrically.

The extremely tiny particles of which atoms and molecules are made have a special property known as *electric charge*, which comes in two varieties:

Alec Jeffreys, a geneticist at the University of Leicester in England, first developed the genetic profiling process.

negative and *positive*. It's difficult to define exactly what electric charge is, except in terms of the way electrically charged particles interact with one another. Particles with like charges (negative and negative or positive and positive) tend to repel one another and particles with opposite charges (negative and positive or positive and negative) tend to attract one another.

If a molecule is made of equal amounts of negatively and positively charged particles, it will have no electric charge itself, because the electric charges of the particles of which it is made precisely cancel out. But if a molecule contains more positively charged particles than negatively charged, or vice versa, then the entire molecule will take on the same charge as the excessive particles. That is, if there is an excess of negatively charged particles, the molecule will have a negative charge. And if there is an excess of positively charged particles, the molecule will have a positive charge.

DNA molecules have an excess of negatively charged particles, so the DNA molecules themselves have a negative charge. For years, scientists have taken advantage of this fact with a process called *gel electrophoresis,* which uses electrical charge to sort pieces of DNA molecule according to size.

In gel electrophoresis, a plate containing a substance known as *agarose* is placed between two electrodes, one of them negatively charged and one of them positively charged. The surface of the plate is divided up into a series of *lanes,* running from the negatively charged side to the positively charged side. At the negatively charged end of each lane is a small well, into which is placed a small sample of DNA molecules.

When current to the electrodes is turned on, the negatively charged DNA molecules are repelled by the negatively charged electrode (because like charges repel) and attracted by the positively charged electrode (because opposite charges attract). As a result, the DNA molecules begin moving out of the wells and toward the positively charged electrode.

But the DNA molecules are not free to fly across the plate and attach themselves' to the positively charged electrode like a paperclip picked up by a horseshoe magnet. To the DNA, the agarose on the plate is like a dense molecular thicket, through which the DNA molecules can move only with difficulty. Smaller DNA molecules can move through the agarose more easily, because they can slide between the agarose molecules. But larger DNA molecules quickly become mired in the agarose and barely move at all.

The result is a kind of DNA horse race, with the smaller DNA molecules proceeding down the agarose-filled lane at a faster clip than the more sluggish large DNA molecules. When the current is turned off and the race comes to an end, the DNA molecules are distributed up and down the lane according to size, with the smallest molecules at the end of the lane nearest the positively charged electrode, the largest molecules at the end of the lane nearest the negatively charged electrode, and the in-between sized molecules somewhere in the middle.

What good does this do? Well, it depends on what the scientist is trying to do. In Jeffreys' case, he was trying to count the number of repeating intron sequences in a fragment of DNA.

Jeffreys used restriction enzymes, as described in the last chapter, to slice specific introns out of a DNA molecule. He then placed the sliced DNA in a well at one end of a gel electrophoresis plate and turned on the current to the electrodes. The DNA fragments began moving down the lanes toward the other end of the plate.

He then turned off the electrodes and placed a sheet of nylon on the gel, letting the DNA molecules soak into the nylon like ink onto a blotter. Once the DNA was transferred to the nylon sheet, he exposed it to *radioactive probes.*

A radioactive probe is a molecule that is specially designed to attach itself to a specific sequence of DNA bases, in this case the bases of the specific DNA fragments that Jeffreys was examining. The DNA distributed along the lane on the electrophoresis plate contained many sequences of bases other than those that Jeffreys wished to compare; thus, the radioactive probes tagged the desired sequences while ignoring the others. And because these probes contain radioactive molecules, they can be detected by a number of methods.

Jeffreys then placed the nylon sheet against a photographic plate and left it there long enough for the plate to become exposed to radiation from the radioactive probes. When he removed and developed the plate, he had a "photograph" of the positions of the DNA fragments on the sheet.

This photograph shows the lanes in the gel electrophoresis plate overlaid with a series of dark stripes (or *bands)*, representing the strips of radioactively tagged DNA fragments lying along the lane. The positions of the dark bands on the plate are determined by the size of the fragments (as described above), and the size of the fragments is in turn determined by the number of times that the intron sequences are repeated in those fragments. Thus, the bands at one end of a lane in the photograph represent larger fragments and the bands at the other end represent smaller fragments. Since the number of repetitions is different for different individuals, the pattern of dark bands will also be different for each individual. These dark bands, which are almost invariably compared to the bar codes found on packages in stores, are the DNA fingerprints.

To compare the "fingerprints" from two pieces of DNA—for example, a piece of DNA taken from a crime suspect and a piece of DNA taken from blood found at the scene of the crime—one piece of DNA is placed in one lane on the gel electrophoresis plate and the other piece is placed in the adjacent lane (Fig. 2). Then the current to the electrodes is turned on and the process described above is executed and a photograph produced, showing the DNA fragments as dark bands in adjacent lanes. If the band in one lane is at the same position as the band in the adjacent lane, then the fragments must be of identical size (and number of intron repetitions) and could have come from the same individual. If the bands are in different positions, then they are of different sizes and must have come from different individuals.

How unique are these fingerprints? Well, say that a specific pattern of repeating sequences in a particular intron is shared by only 10 percent of the people in the world. That means that the band on the DNA fingerprint can be used to determine if the person who contributed the DNA in one lane of the print is in the same 10 percent of the population as the person who contributed the DNA in the other lane. But suppose we add another intron sequence from a different part of the same DNA molecule, adding additional bands to our DNA fingerprints? If *both* bands are in the same place, then we have narrowed down the identification even more closely. If the chance of two individuals having the same pattern of repeating sequences in each fragment are 1 in 10, then the chance of two individuals having the same pattern of repeating sequences in both fragments is 1 in 100.

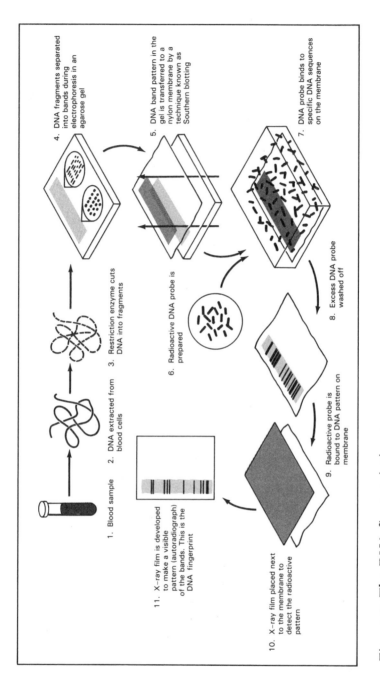

Figure 2. The DNA fingerprinting process

1. Blood sample

2. DNA extracted from blood cells

3. Restriction enzyme cuts DNA into fragments

4. DNA fragments separated into bands during electrophoresis in an agarose gel

5. DNA band pattern in the gel is transferred to a nylon membrane by a technique known as Southern blotting

6. Radioactive DNA probe is prepared

7. DNA probe binds to specific DNA sequences on the membrane

8. Excess DNA probe washed off

9. Radioactive probe is bound to DNA pattern on membrane

10. X-ray film placed next to the membrane to detect the radioactive pattern

11. X-ray film is developed to make a visible pattern (autoradiograph) of the bands. This is the DNA fingerprint

Thus, if this two-band DNA fingerprint is also identical between the two samples of DNA, then we have narrowed the contributor of the bands down to 1 percent of the population.

By adding more and more fragments (and more and more bands) to the DNA fingerprint, we make the fingerprint more and more unique. If we use ten different fragments and the bands from all ten fragments match, then they were almost certainly contributed by the same individual, since the chance of two different people having the same pattern of bands is 1 in 10,000,000,000 (or 1 followed by 10 zeros) if the chance of two individuals having any one band in common is 1 in 10.

Of course, the odds of two people having the same sequence of repeating intron fragments is not always 1 in 10. Sometimes it's 1 in 5 or 1 in 30 or 1 in 100, depending on how many variations of that particular sequence exist in the population. But if we know the odds of any two individuals sharing any one band in the fingerprint in common, then we can calculate the odds of any two individuals sharing *all* of the bands in common by multiplying the odds together for the individual bands. The result is very high odds against two people having the same DNA fingerprint, as long as enough different fragments (or, more properly, *probes* to identify those fragments) are used in creating the fingerprint.

When Jeffreys invented this technique, he immediately saw a number of possibilities inherent in it. Not only could it be used to identify criminals through DNA analysis of blood or hair or semen left at the scene of a crime, but it could be used to establish relationships between parents and children. In a paternity suit, for instance, where a woman charges a reluctant former suitor as the parent of her child, DNA fingerprinting could be used to determine

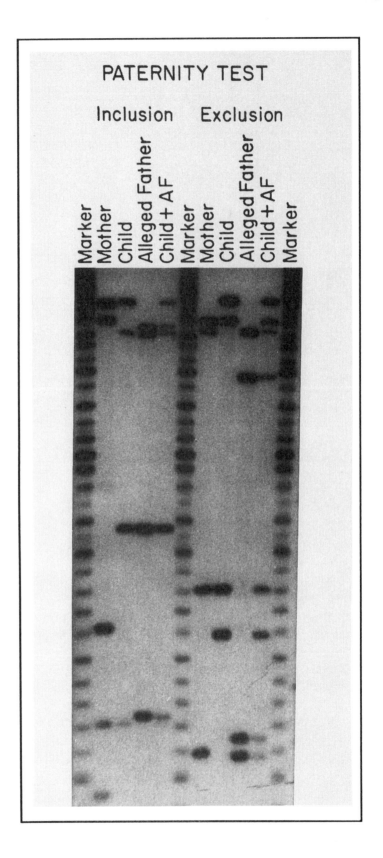

whether the man really was the father of the child. In the past, blood tests had been used for this purpose, because the blood type of the child is based on the blood types of the parents. But the use of blood types to establish parentage is no more accurate than the use of blood types in forensics: it is better used to eliminate possible parents than to prove who the parents actually are. DNA fingerprinting, on the other hand, could prove to be a foolproof method of identifying parent and child when an adequate number of DNA segments are used for this testing. All that needs to be done is to take blood (or some other sample containing DNA) from the mother, the possible father, and the child, and compare them in a DNA fingerprint to see if the child's DNA fingerprint is a combination of the two adults' DNA fingerprints.

It could also be used to settle certain immigration questions. Under British law, foreign citizens can

Application of DNA profiling to a paternity suit. This is a photograph of an autoradiograph used in two different paternity cases. The test (labeled "Inclusion"), at left, *shows DNA from the mother, child, alleged father, and mixture of the child and alleged father. All the DNA bands in the child are present in either the mother or alleged father. This identifies the father as the biological father. In the test,* at right, *the child has a DNA band that is not present in either the mother or the alleged father, and the man is therefore excluded as the biological father.*

immigrate to England if they can prove that they are a direct relative of a British citizen. But proving this relationship is far from easy. Documentation is not always available and eager would-be immigrants have been known to lie about their ancestry to obtain entry.

With Jeffreys' process, though, it is possible to show genetic relationships between individuals by comparing their DNA fingerprints. Although no two individuals have the same genetic makeup or the same genetic fingerprints, the fingerprints of relatives should show distinct similarities and these similarities could be used as proof of the relationship.

To see if the technique worked as he believed it would, Jeffreys tried his DNA fingerprinting technique on the members of a British family and carefully compared their fingerprints. To his delight, common gene patterns ran through all of the fingerprints, just as theory had indicated they should. Jeffreys was thrilled. The technique worked!

Aware that the technique had distinct commercial possibilities, Jeffreys licensed it to a company called Imperial Chemical Industries and began performing DNA fingerprinting for a fee. His first case was an immigration dispute. A young boy from Africa claimed that he had in fact been born in England (though his parents were originally from Ghana). His mother, he said, still lived in England and was a British citizen; the identity of his father was unknown. British authorities, on the other hand, claimed that the woman was not his mother but his aunt.

Could Jeffreys prove that the woman was the boy's mother? This was a tricky case. Jeffreys performed a DNA analysis of the mother and the boy, but no DNA sample of the father was available. The only way Jeffreys could be sure that the mother was in fact the mother and not the aunt was if he had a DNA fingerprint of the father and could show that the boy's DNA fingerprint was a combination of the mother's fingerprint and the father's fingerprint *and no one else's!* Simply showing that the boy shared genes with the woman was not enough; he would share genes with an aunt as well as with his mother.

How could Jeffreys get the father's fingerprint if the father were no longer around? Fortunately, the mother had given birth to several other children by the same man. So Jeffreys performed DNA fingerprinting on all of these children. By subtracting the portion of their fingerprints that matched the mother's, he was able to reconstruct the fingerprint of the missing father. He then showed that the boy's DNA fingerprint was a combination of the fingerprints of the mother and the missing father. The boy was indeed who he claimed to be.

DNA fingerprinting was already beginning to prove itself as a useful technique. But its acceptance as a technique for solving crimes was yet to come. However, the series of crimes that would provide the first testing ground for the forensic possibilities of DNA fingerprinting had already begun.

Perhaps the major drawback of DNA fingerprinting in forensic usage is the fact that the DNA samples commonly found at crime scenes tend to be small. DNA molecules deteriorate rapidly and are often found in dried form—dried blood, dried semen —from which only a relatively small number of intact molecules can be extracted. Or they can become contaminated during or after the commission of the crime, intermingled with DNA or other molecules from the victim or with debris from the surrounding environment.

In a paternity case or an immigration dispute, it is possible to obtain as much DNA as is necessary. If a

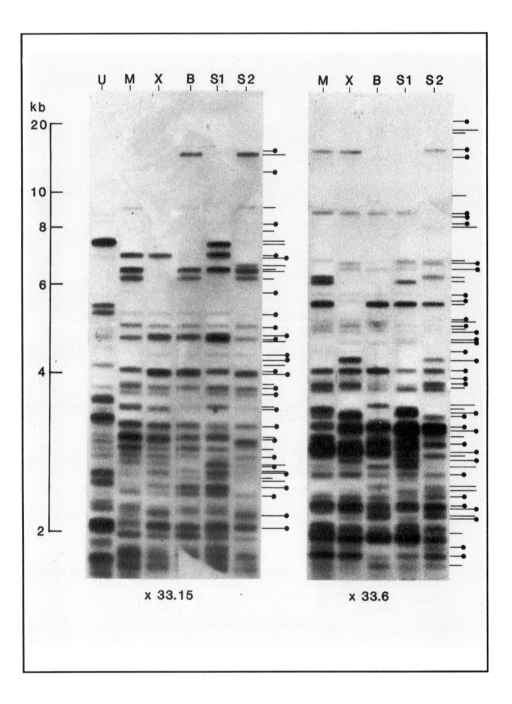

x 33.15   x 33.6

first blood sample proves insufficient, the investigator need only go back and draw more blood. The human body manufactures gallons of the stuff every year.

But samples taken from a crime scene are available in limited quantity. If there's not enough there when the scene is first inspected, there will never be enough. What's needed is a way to amplify a small sample of DNA into a large sample.

Fortunately, techniques for doing just this have been developed, even before Jeffreys' invention of the DNA fingerprinting process itself. Perhaps the most successful of these techniques is the *polymerase chain reaction*, or PCR for short.

PCR was discovered in 1983 by a biochemist named Kary Mullis. Mullis worked for the Cetus Corporation, a biotechnology firm based in California, and was studying human genes in order to find the tiny errors in those genes that cause genetic diseases.

The problem was this: the genes that Mullis

Alec Jeffreys' technique was used in an immigration case to determine whether an African boy was actually a member of a certain family. X represents the boy. The other individuals typed were U, an unrelated individual; M, the mother of the family; B, an undisputed brother in the family; and S1 and S2, undisputed sisters in the family. All markers detected in X can be found in either M, S1, S2, or as a paternal band from the missing father in B. This established that X was a legitimate member of the family, and he was accepted as one of their own.

wanted to study represented no more than the tini-est portion of the human chromosome. Finding that tiny portion was no easy task. And making additional copies of it so that it could be studied with ease was even harder. There were established procedures for doing this, involving the recombinant DNA techniques mentioned in the last chapter. But these procedures were time consuming, taking days or weeks or even months.

On a drive through the California countryside, Mullis suddenly had a better idea. When he returned to the laboratory, he tried it out.

Mullis took the large piece of DNA from which he wanted to isolate a small sequence of bases and put it in a test tube along with two much smaller pieces of DNA called *oligonucleotide primers*. These primers were designed to attach themselves automatically to the larger piece of DNA at both ends of the sequence of bases Mullis wanted to study. He then created proper conditions in the test tube for the DNA to start making copies of itself, just as DNA molecules do when a cell splits into two cells.

The primers acted as a signal to the DNA to start copying itself at that specific point on the molecule, so that the complete molecule was not copied. However, once the molecule started copying itself at the beginning of the desired sequence, there was no way to stop the copying process when the end of the desired sequence was copied, so the copying continued until the end of the molecule was reached. What Mullis ended up with was a copy of the DNA molecule starting with the desired sequence of bases, but running all the way to the other end of the molecule. This was still much too large a piece of DNA for Mullis's purposes, so he then allowed the DNA to make a second copy of itself, this time starting from the primer at the *other* end of the desired sequence of bases. This time, the copying ended when the end of the desired sequence was reached (the point where the previous copy began). Mullis wound up with a copy of *only* the sequence of bases in which he was interested. He then allowed this section of the DNA molecule to copy itself over and over again, until he had literally millions of copies of the sequence. The DNA had been effectively amplified.

The advantage of this method of copying a sequence of bases from a DNA molecule is that it can be easily automated. Over the next four years, Mullis refined the process and built a machine that could perform it automatically. This PCR machine is now standard equipment in many biology laboratories. Any biologist wishing to study a small sequence of bases on a DNA molecule can use the machine to make as many copies of the sequence as he wishes.

Laboratories interested in performing DNA fingerprinting quickly realized that PCR was the ideal method of "amplifying" genetic evidence found at the scene of a crime. Even if only a small amount of DNA is available—a single hair, for instance—the intron sequences in that DNA can be multiplied many times by PCR, allowing forensic scientists to study that sequence to their heart's content.

And, indeed, there were a number of laboratories interested in using the technique that Alec Jeffreys had developed. In the United States, for instance, most of the DNA fingerprinting work is now performed at two commercial laboratories, Lifecodes Inc. and Cellmark. The FBI also has a DNA fingerprinting laboratory.

In theory, DNA fingerprinting is a powerful forensic technique. But how does it work in practice? Let's look at some examples of DNA fingerprinting in action and see just how important it can be in the solving of crimes.

FOUR
THE FIRST CASES

The body was discovered by a hospital porter on his way to work. It lay on the ground, in the early morning dew, just outside the grounds of a mental hospital in Narborough, England. It was the morning of November 22, 1983. Five thousand miles away, in the United States, Americans were observing the twentieth anniversary of the assassination of President John F. Kennedy, but in Narborough a four-year-long manhunt was only just beginning.

The body belonged to a fifteen-year-old girl named Lynda Mann. She had lived with her mother, sister, and stepfather, not far from where her corpse was discovered. Police forensic experts, who were called in not long after the body was discovered, determined that she had been raped and strangled.

Although it was not immediately evident who had killed Lynda Mann—and would not be evident for another four years—the killer and rapist had left something behind, a small sample of his semen. It would be that sample of semen, and another that he would leave behind on the body of another girl three years later, that would eventually provide the clue that would solve the crime.

Small English towns like Narborough are not often the scene of violent murders. And Lynda Mann had been a well-liked young woman from a respectable family. Inevitably her death caused a stir in the community and the police were urged to devote all of their resources to catching her killer.

A massive manhunt began. Eyewitness reports began arriving at police headquarters of spike-haired punkers seen fleeing the area of the crime on the evening of November 21, when Lynda was apparently killed, but these reports came to nothing. The patients at the mental hospital were interviewed, but none seemed likely to be the killer. An analysis of the semen found on Lynda's body revealed a high sperm count, which indicated that a relatively young man had committed the rape—so all men between the ages of fourteen and thirty-four in Narborough and surrounding communities were interviewed to determine if they had alibis for the evening that the murder had been committed. More than a few men in this age group had no alibi, but there was no way to tie any of them to the scene of the crime.

A year after Lynda Mann's body was found, the crime was still unsolved. Police still sifted clues and followed leads, hoping for a break that would lead them to the young girl's murderer. But luck was not with them. The killer still had not been caught.

Then, on July 31, 1986, another fifteen-year-old girl disappeared, this time in the nearby village of Enderby. A search was organized and on the morning of August 2, the body of Dawn Ashworth was found near a path leading through the woods that separated Enderby from Narborough. Like Lynda Mann three years earlier, Dawn Ashworth had been raped and strangled.

The resemblances between the two crimes were too obvious to ignore. Both girls were fifteen years old, both had been raped, both had been killed in the same manner, and both bodies were found within a few miles of each other. It was clear to the police that they were dealing with a serial killer: The same man must have raped and killed both girls.

The Lynda Mann case had grown cold long before, but now police felt they had a second chance to solve it. If they could find the killer of Dawn Ashworth, they would also find the killer of Lynda Mann, assuming as they did that the same man had committed both crimes.

Another manhunt was organized and this time the police got the break that they needed. They learned that a young dishwasher who lived in Enderby had told a friend about the discovery of Dawn Ashworth's body several hours before the discovery was publicly announced. Further, the young man apparently knew several details about the condition of the body, even though they were not public knowledge.

Although still a teenager, the dishwasher was a large young man, six feet (1.8 m) tall and solidly built. He was also something of a village character. Not terribly bright and perhaps mentally unstable, the dishwasher had a habit of making forcible sexual advances on young girls, sneaking up behind them and slipping his hand under their dresses. To the police, he seemed an ideal candidate for the murderer of Dawn Ashworth and Lynda Mann.

The dishwasher was arrested and subjected to a lengthy police interview. At first he denied any connection with the crime, but after extensive questioning he began to confess haltingly to the murder of Dawn Ashworth. The confession was incoherent and frequently contradictory, but it seemed clear to the police that they had arrested the murderer of Dawn Ashworth.

Yet, to their frustration, the dishwasher refused to confess to the earlier murder of Lynda Mann. If, as the police firmly believed, the same person had murdered both girls, then the dishwasher must be Lynda Mann's murderer as well as Dawn Ashworth's. But, in the absence of a confession, they had no concrete way of tying the young man to the scene of the earlier crime.

It was at this point that one of the policemen in charge of the investigation had an inspiration. He had read in a magazine about a new forensic technique called DNA fingerprinting. It had not yet been used to solve a crime, but it seemed like an ideal technique for proving the dishwasher's guilt. They could send a sample of the dishwasher's blood to a testing laboratory along with the semen samples found on the bodies of Lynda Mann and Dawn Ashworth and show conclusively that the dishwasher had committed both crimes!

Alec Jeffreys, the inventor of the DNA fingerprinting technique, was contacted and given the semen and blood samples. He then analyzed them, comparing the DNA fingerprints of the semen found on Lynda Mann and the semen found on Dawn Ashworth with the DNA fingerprint of the blood taken from the dishwasher.

The result? The DNA from the semen found on Lynda Mann did *not* match the DNA in the dishwasher's blood. So the dishwasher was in fact telling the truth; he had not committed the earlier murder. The police were now back to square one on that crime.

But, from the viewpoint of the police, there was worse news yet to come. The DNA from the semen found on Dawn Ashworth didn't match the DNA from the dishwasher's blood, either. Despite his confession, the dishwasher hadn't committed that crime.

The Narborough police had mixed feelings about the forensic debut of DNA fingerprinting. The new technique had just set them back three years in the solution of the Lynda Mann murder.

On the other hand, it had saved an innocent teenager from prison.

Jeffreys's DNA fingerprints also verified the police theory that the same person had committed both murders. The DNA fingerprints from the semen found on the two bodies, murdered three years apart, matched perfectly!

The police reasoned that if DNA fingerprinting could prove the innocence of one suspect, it could help them catch another. The Narborough police department thus conceived one of the most dramatic schemes in the history of forensic science. They decided that they would draw the blood of every young man in Narborough and Enderby who could reasonably be suspected of having murdered Dawn Ashworth or Lynda Mann and compare their DNA fingerprints with those of the semen found on the bodies.

In December 1986, the police began "bloodying" the suspects, as they liked to call it. Those men who were of the right age to have murdered the two girls and who lacked an airtight alibi for the evenings on which the murders occurred were called in one by one to the Narborough police station, where samples of their blood were taken.

Months passed and hundreds of DNA fingerprints were taken from the blood samples given to the Narborough police. And yet none of them matched the DNA fingerprints from the semen found on the bodies of the two girls! By the summer of 1987, a full year after the murder of Dawn Ashworth, not a single suspect had been uncovered despite the massive campaign of DNA fingerprinting.

And then the big break came. A young woman who managed a local bakery called the police to tell them of a conversation she had had with companions in a local pub. One of the men at her table had confessed that another man had paid him to go to the Narborough police station and give blood in his name. The man who had paid this fellow to give blood was named Colin Pitchfork.

The police were already aware of Pitchfork. He was a flasher, a man who liked to expose his genitals to unsuspecting female passersby, and had been arrested several times for indecent exposure. He had been interviewed four years earlier, after the murder of Lynda Mann, and had no alibi for the night when the girl had been killed. But no evidence had ever been found to link him with the crime. And when police had drawn blood from "Pitchfork" and analyzed his DNA fingerprint, it had not matched the fingerprint of the semen found on the murder victim.

But now it appeared that the man who had given blood to the police was not Pitchfork at all, but another man whom Pitchfork had paid to appear at the police station in his place. Why would Pitchfork have gone to such trouble to avoid giving blood? Clearly he must be the killer!

The police waited until they were sure that Pitchfork was home, then they surrounded his house and knocked on his front door. His wife answered. Pitchfork appeared a few moments later and the police confronted him with their accusation. So confident was Pitchfork that the DNA fingerprint would reveal his guilt that he confessed to both murders on the spot.

And when Colin Pitchfork's blood was finally

drawn and analyzed, his DNA fingerprint was identical to those taken from the semen found on the bodies of Lynda Mann and Dawn Ashworth.

The Lynda Mann–Dawn Ashworth case proved to be a dramatic showcase for the DNA fingerprinting technique. It was publicized around the world and drew considerable attention to this new forensic technology. Police in the United States and several other countries watched carefully to see if this technique could be useful for cases that they were having trouble solving.

But the law moves in strange and subtle ways. Before DNA fingerprinting could be accepted in the courts as proof of a defendant's guilt, it would need to be accepted by judges, who are often reluctant to admit a new and untried method of gathering evidence into their courtrooms. There was no precedent for the use of DNA fingerprinting, and unless some innovative prosecutors were willing to take the chance that carefully gathered DNA evidence would be thrown out of court by an unimpressed judge, there never would be.

In the case of Colin Pitchfork, the DNA evidence was not necessary for his conviction as a murderer. Pitchfork had confessed to his crimes in extensive and vivid detail. (Some even suggested that Pitchfork was proud of what he had done and wanted to brag about it to the police.) But other suspects might not be so forthcoming.

And it is unlikely that many police forces are in a position to mount the sort of massive bloodtesting campaign that the Narborough police engaged in to catch their man. In the United States especially, where civil rights are carefully guarded, it seems highly unlikely that any community would accept such an invasive technique of smoking out a killer.

DNA fingerprinting nonetheless has a place in

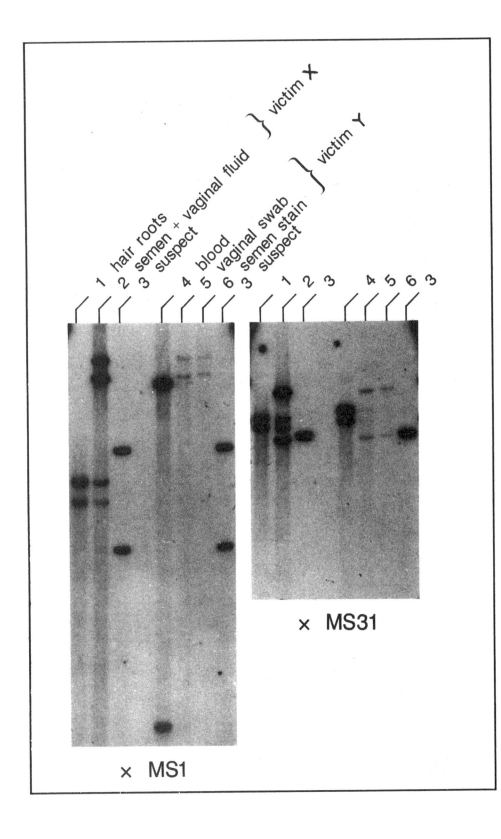

crimefighting in the United States. In fact, it was only a year after the Narborough police caught Colin Pitchfork that police in the United States began adding DNA fingerprinting to their own arsenal of forensic techniques.

In August 1987, the chief prosecutor of Orange County, Florida, was in a quandary. He was convinced that Tommie Lee Andrews was the man responsible for breaking into homes and raping several women in the Orlando area. Although the rapist had taken pains to avoid being seen by the women he had attacked—usually, he would cover a woman's head with a sheet before he assaulted her—one of the women had managed to get a good look at his face and was prepared to identify Andrews as the man she had seen. And yet the prosecutor wasn't sure that he had enough evidence to convict Andrews in court.

The prosecutor, Tim Berry, related his problem to a lawyer named Jeffrey Ashton, who mentioned a report he'd seen on television about how DNA fingerprinting had been used to catch Colin Pitchfork in England. Ashton had also seen an ad in a legal magazine for a company called Lifecodes, Inc., that

DNA fingerprinting results used to investigate the rape and murder of both Lynda Mann and Dawn Ashforth. Two different DNA probes were made. The results indicated that both girls had probably been raped, and therefore also murdered, by the same man. That man was, curiously enough, originally not the prime suspect.

would perform DNA fingerprinting to order. He suggested that Berry give them a call.

Intrigued, Berry contacted Lifecodes and arranged for them to analyze a sample of semen taken from one of the rape victims and compare it to DNA from a sample of Andrews's blood. Lifecodes performed the comparison and announced that the samples matched. There was no doubt; Andrews was the rapist. Lifecodes further announced that there was only one chance in 10 billion of another person having the same fingerprint, based on the frequency with which the DNA fragments analyzed by Lifecodes appeared in the population.

In October 1987, the Andrews case went to court. He was charged with the rape of the twenty-seven-year-old woman who had seen his face and identified him for police. Tim Berry, the prosecutor, was prepared to use the DNA fingerprinting evidence in court to prove that Andrews was indeed the rapist, even though DNA fingerprinting had never before been used in a criminal case in the United States.

To support his case, he had arranged for several expert witnesses to appear at the trial. One was a molecular biologist from the Massachusetts Institute of Technology (MIT) named David Housman, who would give the judge and jury a lesson in genetics theory. Another was Michael Baird, director of forensic and paternity testing at Lifecodes. If all went well, these witnesses would convince the jury that the testimony of the DNA fingerprints was incontrovertible evidence against the accused.

Things did not go as planned. Housman gave his speech on genetics and Baird took the witness stand to testify that there was only one chance in 10 billion that the semen taken from the rape victim did not come from Andrews.

But the defense lawyer immediately objected that

there was no precedent for the use of such technology in court. Neither Berry nor Baird was immediately able to address this objection. Flustered, Berry withdrew the DNA fingerprinting evidence. When the jury was not able to reach a verdict, a mistrial was declared.

The trials of Tommie Lee Andrews were not yet over, however. Andrews was to be tried again in two weeks for the assault of another of his alleged victims and Berry had arranged for a retrial of the first case after the declaration of a mistrial. Things went more smoothly during the second trial; the objections of the defense lawyers were answered with legal precedents that Berry had uncovered in the interim, and the jury accepted the evidence. Andrews was convicted. And when the first victim's case was retried in February 1988, Andrews was convicted again. The DNA fingerprinting evidence had won acceptance.

In the wake of these two convictions—Colin Pitchfork's in the United Kingdom and Tommie Lee Andrews's in the United States—DNA fingerprinting came into its own. It was rapidly adopted by forensics experts around the world. Case after case came to trial with DNA fingerprinting evidence prepared against the defendant, though over and over again it was necessary for judges to decide whether this evidence was indeed admissible.

By 1989, it looked as though DNA fingerprinting were the most spectacularly effective new forensic technique ever discovered. And yet some doubts remained. Perhaps DNA fingerprinting was being overhyped. Perhaps some flaws remained in the technique.

In the summer of 1989, those flaws were dramatically revealed in a pair of cases that nearly halted the use of DNA fingerprinting in criminal trials!

61

FIVE
SECOND THOUGHTS

In theory, the DNA fingerprinting technique sounds foolproof. Put one sample of DNA in one lane of the electrophoresis plate, another sample in another lane, and turn on the electrodes. A few hours, and a few steps later, you'll have a photograph showing a series of easily identifiable bands in each lane that can be infallibly compared to verify the source of the DNA.

And if the DNA taken from the scene of a crime produces the same set of bands as the DNA taken from a suspect, the crime is solved.

In practice, however, the technique doesn't work quite this smoothly. As we noted earlier, evidence found at the scene of a crime can become contaminated, which may lead to strange bands appearing in some of the lanes. DNA samples can also become degraded over time, often before police can arrive at the scene of a crime, and the resulting fingerprint may lack bands that would normally be vital for identification. Small differences in position between bands in adjacent lanes, representing slightly differer-t sized pieces of DNA, are difficult to distinguish on a DNA fingerprint. And sometimes the bands in one of the lanes on the plate can mysteriously move to the left or right, making it difficult to compare the bands in one lane with the bands in the other.

This last phenomenon is known as *band-shift.* What causes it? No one is quite sure. All that is known is that sometimes one of the lanes on the electrophoresis plate will "run faster" than the other lanes. DNA in that lane will proceed from one electrode to the other at a faster pace than identical pieces of DNA in the other lanes. Perhaps this has something to do with the way in which the gel on the plate was prepared, or with the amount of DNA placed in each of the wells, or even with contamination of the DNA.

Even when band-shifting occurs, however, it is still possible to compare two lanes in a DNA fingerprint. An expert can look at the fingerprint and recognize that the pattern of bands in each lane are the same, even if one pattern is shifted relative to the other. But this adds a measure of human subjectivity to a technique that has been touted as an objective method of determining guilt or innocence. The future of a possibly innocent human being rests on the results of the DNA fingerprinting analysis, and an educated guess is a far cry from the 1-in-10 billion accuracy claimed for DNA fingerprints in cases such as the Tommie Lee Andrews trial discussed in the last chapter.

Fortunately, there is a more objective method of identifying a band-shifted lane in a DNA fingerprint. Not all fragments of human DNA vary as widely from one individual to another as the introns commonly used in DNA fingerprinting. Many fragments are virtually identical in all human beings. Radioactive probes for these fragments are called *monomorphic* (one-shape) *probes*. By adding some of these monomorphic probes to the DNA fingerprint, a series of *control bands* will appear. These bands should be identical in each lane. If they are shifted, then band-shifting has clearly occurred. Furthermore, the shift in these bands can be measured and used to adjust all of the other bands.

In theory, this should solve the problem of band-shifting. In practice, however, there are still problems.

In 1989, the problems associated with DNA finger-printing surfaced in a pair of well-publicized cases. As a result, questions were raised about the way in which DNA fingerprinting was being used as evidence in criminal cases, and the future of DNA fingerprinting as a forensic technique was suddenly put in doubt.

José Castro, a Hispanic immigrant living in New York and working as a handyman, stood accused of the vicious murder of a woman named Vilma Ponce and her two-year-old daughter. There had been a witness to the murder, but the pivotal piece of physical evidence linking Castro to the crime was a bloodstain found on Castro's wristwatch. The Bronx District Attorney's office had sent a sample taken from this bloodstain to Lifecodes, Inc., for DNA fingerprinting, along with a sample of Vilma Ponce's blood. They received in return a conclusive report: the blood on Castro's watch was the blood of Vilma Ponce. Based on the frequency that the various genetic fragments used by Lifecodes occurred in the Hispanic community in which the murder had taken place, the company estimated that there was only 1 chance in 100 million of a mistake.

This figure sounded pretty intimidating to Castro's defense attorney, so he made an unusual decision, one that would eventually have far-reaching repercussions for the use of DNA fingerprinting. He challenged the reliability of the DNA fingerprinting technique itself. At first, this challenge took the form of a request for a Frye hearing. But soon the Castro case would become a sort of miniature scientific conference, where scientists would get together and argue the case for DNA fingerprinting among themselves, as the Castro case hung in the balance.

The Frye hearings had grown out of a 1923 case in the District of Columbia known as *Frye* versus *U.S.* In that case, the Court of Appeals had been asked to accept evidence obtained through the use of an early version of the lie detector. The evidence was rejected and the court's statement on the admissibility of scientifically grounded evidence had constituted an important legal precedent. That statement, in part, had read: "Just when a scientific principle crosses the line between the experimental and demonstrable stages is difficult to define. Somewhere in this twilight zone the evidential force of the principle must be recognized and while courts will go a long way in admitting expert testimony deduced from a well-recognized scientific principle or discovery, the thing from which the deduction is made must be sufficiently established to have gained general acceptance in the particular field in which it belongs."[1]

At a Frye hearing, expert scientific witnesses argue the case, both pro and con, for a new forensic technology. But the basis of the Frye hearing has been challenged over the years by scientists and lawyers alike. The criteria used at a Frye hearing to

[1] Peter J. Neufeld and Neville Colman, "When Science Takes the Witness Stand," *Scientific American,* May 1990, p. 48.

decide whether scientific evidence should be admissible in court have been called vague and unsatisfactory. Worst of all from the viewpoint of many scientists, the Frye hearing uses an adversarial system for deciding whether or not a scientific technique is valid—that is, experts on both sides of the issue (and often on both sides of a criminal case) argue back and forth, each expert trying to win a victory for his or her side (which is usually the side that is paying the expert to take that position).

Scientists often settle issues of their own in an adversarial manner, but they do so (ideally, at least) as part of a quest for truth, not in order to gain a victory out of selfish interests. A scientist who has been proven wrong will usually admit having been mistaken and will often join the opposition, championing the theory that he or she once opposed; this rarely happens in a courtroom.

Castro's defense lawyer contacted Peter Neufeld and Barry Scheck, a pair of lawyers with an interest in the DNA fingerprinting techniques. Neufeld and Scheck had recently attended a conference on the subject and were having misgivings about the techniques. While at the conference, the lawyers had met Eric Lander, a geneticist and mathematician from the Whitehead Institute in Cambridge, Massachusetts. Lander had watched several presentations at the conference where experts from Lifecodes and Cellmark had demonstrated their forensic work, and the presentations had struck Landers as sloppy.

For instance, in one demonstration a Lifecodes expert had shown the audience a fingerprint consisting of two lanes and declared that the two lanes matched, although the bands in one lane were not in the same positions as the bands in the other. The expert argued that band-shifting had occurred between the two lanes, but offered no objective scientific criteria for correcting the band-shifting. In another presentation, an expert from Cellmark had declared that two seemingly dissimilar lanes in a fingerprint matched and blamed the dissimilarity on degradation of the DNA.

Landers was not impressed, and the two lawyers were persuaded that DNA fingerprinting techniques needed to be examined in more detail if they were to become a staple of forensic technology. Clearly, standard criteria were needed in the forensic use of DNA fingerprinting and there was no evidence that companies such as Lifecodes and Cellmark were using such criteria. To the contrary, many of the decisions as to whether two fingerprints did or did not match seemed to be made on intuitive grounds—by educated guesswork—rather than with any kind of scientific precision.

When Neufeld and Scheck were contacted by Castro's lawyer, they in turn contacted Eric Lander and asked him if he was willing to testify as an expert witness. Perhaps he could cast some doubt on the use of DNA fingerprinting in the case. Lander was reluctant at first, but eventually agreed. Then a fateful coincidence occurred. Lander, who was now an expert witness for the defense, was at a scientific conference when he met a fellow scientist who turned out to be an expert witness for the prosecution. The second scientist was Richard Roberts, a molecular biologist at Cold Spring Harbor Laboratory in New York, who was scheduled to testify at the trial in favor of the DNA fingerprinting techniques.

The two scientists began talking and realized that they both had qualms about the use of DNA fingerprinting. They then made an unprecedented move: with the cooperation of lawyers for both sides, they contacted the judge and arranged for the Frye hearing to be canceled. Instead, the two scientists asked to be given permission to review the DNA evidence outside the courtroom and make an objective, nonadversarial decision about its validity. Permission was granted.

The meeting was held in a lawyer's office in New York. The scientists examined the report from Lifecodes that showed that the blood on José Castro's watch came from Vilma Ponce, with a 1 in 189,200,000 margin of error. And they didn't like what they saw.

After the meeting, Lander and Roberts issued a public statement: "The data in this case are not scientifically reliable enough to support the assertion that the samples . . . do or do not match. If these data were submitted to a peer-reviewed journal in support of a conclusion, they would not be accepted."[2]

What was wrong with the DNA evidence? The match between the DNA fingerprint taken from Vilma Ponce's blood and the fingerprint taken from the bloodstain on José Castro's watch was far from perfect. On careful examination, two of the bands did not quite match. And there were two bands on the bloodstain fingerprint that were not on Vilma Ponce's fingerprint. Where did these extra bands come from? Lifecodes believed that they were some sort of contamination, perhaps from bacteria, that had entered the bloodstain before the sample was taken. But there was no way to prove that this was so.

Furthermore, the scientists disagreed with Lifecode's estimate that there was only 1 chance in

---

[2] Shawna Vogel, "The Case of the Unraveling DNA," *Discover,* January 1990.

189,200,000 that their conclusion was wrong. This figure was based on the frequency with which the genetic fragments tested by Lifecodes appeared in the DNA of Hispanics in general. But this failed to take into account that certain subgroups of Hispanics (or any other ethnic population) tend to intermarry among themselves, thus increasing the chance that several people within that subgroup might have closely matching DNA fingerprints. The DNA fingerprints of Cubans and Puerto Ricans, for instance, may resemble one another to a greater degree than the DNA fingerprints of Hispanics in general. Thus, the odds of a mistake may be greater than Lifecodes had suggested. What was needed was a careful study of population statistics and genetic variation within populations.

Lifecodes stood by their results (which were obtained in 1987, early in Lifecode's existence), but the judge ruled that the evidence was inadmissible. For the first time since the technique had been developed, a shadow had been cast over the use of DNA fingerprinting in the courts.

The reputation of DNA fingerprinting was further damaged by a case that came to trial in the fall of 1989. This time, a man was accused of having sexually assaulted a five-year-old girl in back of a school in Maine. The prosecution found themselves with a difficult argument: the man did not match the description of the assailant given by the victim and her young companions.

The prosecution did, however, have a singularly damning piece of evidence. A DNA fingerprint taken from the blood of the suspect matched that taken from a sample of semen found at the scene of the crime, according to a forensic report from Lifecodes. (An earlier suspect, who had more closely matched the description of the assailant, had been exonerated when his DNA fingerprint did not match that of the semen sample.)

Under cross-examination in court, however, the DNA evidence began to crumble. The bands in the defendant's DNA fingerprint did not match the bands in the fingerprint taken from the semen sample. Michael Baird, from Lifecodes, argued that band-shifting had taken place and showed that there was evidence that this was so. Lifecodes had used a monomorphic probe as a control and it was shifted just as the other bands were.

The lawyer for the defense, however, pointed out that the company had also used a second control—a fragment of DNA taken from the so-called Y chromosome—and it was shifted by a different amount than the other probe, indicating that the other bands did not in fact match. Baird argued that the second control was not a control at all, but simply a test to determine whether the DNA samples had come from a man or a woman. (Women do not have a Y chromosome; thus its presence indicates that the DNA sample comes from a male donor.) The defense lawyer argued in turn that while the second probe may not have been intended as a control, it nonetheless served as one, and that it indicated the first control might be incorrect.

The judge agreed that the evidence was inconclusive and ruled it inadmissible. The prosecution was forced to drop its charges against the defendant.

Have these cases sounded the death knell for DNA fingerprinting? Not likely. Even opponents of the technique, such as lawyer Peter Neufeld, admit that it is a valuable forensic tool. But there has been little objective scientific study of DNA fingerprinting. Almost no articles on the technique have appeared in refereed scientific journals, where scientists can argue the merits of DNA fingerprinting in an open forum. The development of the technology has taken place largely within the forensic science community, rather than among the larger community of biologists, and many of those working on developing the technique have a financial interest in its success.

Further, standards are needed so that sloppy laboratory work can be avoided. And there must be some objective method for deciding whether or not two DNA fingerprints match; simple "eyeball" estimates will not suffice. Unfortunately, most of the techniques used by companies such as Lifecodes and Cellmark are proprietary—that is, the companies have patented the techniques so that no one else can use them and profit financially from them. As a result, it is virtually impossible to standardize the techniques.

Neufeld argues that the aura of scientific rigor surrounding the DNA fingerprinting technology intimidates both juries and defense lawyers, who don't realize how great the margin of error for such laboratory techniques can sometimes be. A defense lawyer faced with results that have "1 chance in 10 billion" of being wrong may simply shrug and give up; yet such impressive statements of accuracy may be greatly exaggerated. (One scientist estimated that the evidence in a particular case involving DNA fingerprinting probably had closer to 1 chance in 24 of being wrong, not 1 chance in 10 billion.)

In the summer of 1990, a case came to trial in Ohio that may have far-reaching implications for DNA fingerprinting. The defendants are three members of the Hell's Angels motorcycle gang, who are charged with murdering another man they believed to be a member of a rival gang, the Outlaws. A key piece of evidence in the case is a DNA fingerprint that matches blood taken from one of the defendants with blood found in the victim's van.

The judge in this case is an expert in the field of technology and the law, especially where it applies to electronic surveillance. Because the precedent set in this case may affect the outcome of trials all over the United States in which DNA fingerprinting is used as evidence, the government has called in some of its top science experts to testify for the prosecution and the defense has amassed its own team of a dozen experts to testify in opposition. We'll have more to say about this case in the next chapter.

It may bode well for DNA fingerprinting, however, that a study conducted at Yale University in 1990 has found that figures used by Lifecodes and other organizations concerning the probability of two people having the same fingerprint are probably quite accurate. Although many opponents of DNA fingerprinting have argued that these figures may not be true of small subpopulations within larger subpopulations (such as Cubans or Puerto Ricans within the population of Hispanics), the Yale study shows that even in such small subpopulations the odds against two people having accidentally matching fingerprints are still quite large, on the order of 1 in 500,000.

In the next chapter, we'll look again at the issue of accuracy in DNA fingerprinting technology. But we'll also look at another important social issue surrounding this technology: the question of the individual's right to privacy.

SIX
SOCIAL ISSUES

For a moment, let's set aside the issue of whether DNA fingerprinting is as accurate as is claimed by its proponents. In fact, let's assume that it turns out to be a nearly foolproof method of identifying the perpetrator of a crime, assuming that the perpetrator has been gracious enough to leave a sample of his or her DNA at the scene of the crime in a clearly incriminating location.

Certainly this makes DNA fingerprinting an invaluable tool in the never-ending war against crime. And certainly we can all agree that stopping crime is such a valuable goal in itself that we should do everything in our power to achieve it.

Or should we?

In fact, the history of crime-fighting is littered with situations in which the goals of the crime fighter have come into conflict with the goals of society at large. That's why the Bill of Rights—the first ten amendments to the Constitution of the United States —clearly prohibits unreasonable searches and seizures and self-incrimination. That's why the police must have a warrant before they can enter your home, even if they have reason to believe that a crime was committed there. That's why you can choose not to be interrogated about a crime until a lawyer is present to advise you of your legal rights.

Those legal rights are intended to protect the innocent, not the guilty, though they sometimes make it easier for the guilty to go free. The legal rights of a United States citizen are based on the concept that it's better for a guilty person to go free than for an innocent person to be punished unfairly. When a new method of fighting crime begins to infringe on the rights of the innocent, it's time to examine that method carefully to see if the benefits that it provides are worth the social problems that it could cause.

Does DNA fingerprinting infringe on the rights of the innocent? In some ways, the answer is no. The potential precision of the process could actually benefit an innocent party accused of a crime, by conclusively showing that the person could *not* have committed it. But that precision is only potential. Several prominent biologists have gone on record as saying that, if they were innocent of a crime such as rape, they would absolutely *not* want their innocence "tested for" by DNA fingerprinting because the possibility for error is just too great. They might well find themselves convicted by a jury that did not understand how easily errors can be made in the interpretation of DNA evidence.

But this is a scientific argument more than a social argument. It revolves around the question of the accuracy of DNA fingerprinting and the interpretation of DNA fingerprints. Presumably these are problems that can be worked out after sufficient research has been invested in the question of forensic DNA typing. Even if DNA fingerprinting is less than accurate now (and this is still debatable), it presumably will be much more accurate in the near future.

And yet, even if the process is made 99.99999999 percent accurate, there is still a potential for the technique to be abused.

Suppose that at some time in the near future, an overzealous politician announces that it's time to create libraries of genetic information, libraries that will contain the DNA fingerprints of every man, woman, and child in the United States so that DNA found at the scene of a crime can be instantly matched with that of the perpetrator. This sort of genetic library has already been seriously suggested by those with a well-meaning interest in fighting the burgeoning crime problem in the United States. But there are problems inherent in the idea.

What form would such a library take? Well, it could be modeled on existing fingerprint libraries, which record fingerprint information in a short, coded form that can be manipulated by computer. Computers can match fingerprints rapidly, even when fingerprint information is punched in on a remote terminal many thousands of miles away from the fingerprint library itself.

Similarly, DNA fingerprint libraries could contain coded information about DNA fingerprints in such a way that the fingerprints could be matched by computer. This would require that DNA fingerprints be taken of every citizen of the United States—a massive undertaking in itself—then punched into the computer.

Even if the logistical problems of gathering this information were overcome, there would still be a drawback to this method, however. There are several different methods for performing DNA fingerprinting and doubtlessly more will be developed in the future. The information in such an electronic library would quickly become out-of-date. It would be necessary to repeat the process of gathering the genetic information all over again, which really isn't feasible.

The alternative would be to store a specimen of the actual DNA of every citizen in a repository—in the form of a blood sample, perhaps, or a fragment of tissue or even a hank of hair—from which tiny pieces of those specimens could be drawn from time to time to create a state-of-the-art computer library of DNA fingerprints. In this manner, the library could be kept abreast of new techniques. It would never become outdated.

Come to think of it, as long as the DNA specimens are available, there's no reason to stop at using them simply for DNA fingerprints. There's lots of valuable information locked up in a person's DNA, information that could tell us important things about that person.

And that's where the problems begin. A DNA repository would hold far more than just DNA fingerprint information. It would hold a kind of life history of the person who contributed the DNA, a life history stretching not only back into the past but ahead into the future. Properly analyzed, a DNA sample can tell us the sex and race of its bearer, the color of the person's hair and eyes, and every genetic disease that the person is predisposed to—in the past, present, and future. There's even a chance that, at some time in the future, it will be possible to analyze a person's DNA and learn something about that person's personality: whether they are outgoing or withdrawn, Democrat or Republican, heterosexual or gay. Nobody yet knows the sum total of the mysteries contained in DNA, but scientists are slowly learning to read the human DNA like a book. And if repositories of DNA samples become common, those repositories may turn out to contain more information about the citizens of the United States than any government has a right to know.

At present, biologists are just learning to read the evidence of genetic disease in the book of the chromosomes. It is already possible to pinpoint the presence of certain illnesses in a sample of DNA, illnesses that may not yet have manifested themselves in the person from whom the DNA was taken.

What is a genetic illness? Not all genes contain recipes for "good" enzymes. Some genes have, over millions of years of evolution, become corrupted. The enzymes that they produce are defective. In some cases, they are unable to produce enzymes at all.

Usually, when a gene becomes corrupted, the organism carrying that gene dies before it can pass that gene on to its offspring. Thus, the gene is neatly eliminated from the population and can cause no further trouble.

But there are certain circumstances under which a defective gene can survive for many generations, causing illness in its wake. One of these is when the gene doesn't cause problems until a person is older and has already passed the gene on to later generations. In most cases, the individuals don't even realize that they are carrying a defective gene until they fall ill.

A doctor who could "read" a person's genes in such a way as to detect the defective gene could actually foretell that person's future. In some cases, this would do no good at all. Assuming that there's no cure for the genetic disease, the person would have to live with the terrible knowledge that they were going to die an untimely death, perhaps a particularly unpleasant one. In other cases, where a treatment for the disease may be available, the person carrying the defective gene could take precautions early in life to ward off later disease.

Not all defective genes inevitably cause disease. Some merely "predispose" the carrier to illness. But other defective genes are effectively a death sentence for the individual bearing them.

One such gene is that for Huntington's chorea, a degenerative disease that strikes men and women generally between the ages of thirty-five and fifty. As far as doctors and biologists have been able to tell, Huntington's is carried on a single gene on a single chromosome. Individuals who inherit this gene will inevitably die of Huntington's, unless something else kills them first. And the death is not a particularly pleasant one. Huntington's wears down the patients' resistance over a period of ten or fifteen years, gradually reducing their mental faculties until they are unable to care for themselves or go about anything resembling a normal life.

Biologists have searched for the location of the Huntington's gene in the human genome for some years and they are very close to finding it. In fact, they have already learned which chromosome the Huntington's gene is on and have even found *markers*— fragments of DNA known to lie close to the Huntington's gene on that chromosome—that can be used to identify the presence of the Huntington's gene with better than 90 percent accuracy. By analyzing the DNA of a person who may carry the Huntington's gene (as identified by the fact that one of the person's parents carried the Huntington's gene) and looking for these markers, they can predict whether that person will eventually develop Huntington's chorea. In effect, they can predict how that person will die.

This is a frightening yet valuable kind of knowledge. The test is available on a voluntary basis to anyone with a family history of Huntington's. It can lift a great weight off people's minds by letting them know that they are not going to die of the same disease that killed their father or mother. But it can also provide the depressing information that they are only a few years away from slow death. Understandably, only a small number of those people at risk for Huntington's have chosen to take this test.

Huntington's isn't the only disease carried in the human genes. In fact, as biologists learn more and more about our genes, they are discovering that more and more diseases are genetic. There is evidence, for instance, that certain forms of cancer, certain forms of heart disease, and even certain forms of mental illness may have genetic components— that is, certain genes may predispose an individual toward these ailments, often quite strongly.

Scientists still have a great deal to learn about how to read this information from the genes. In most cases, they don't even know where the genes that code for these diseases are located in the genome, just that the genes exist. But, one by one, they are closing in on these genes. Within the next few decades, the locations in the human genome of hundreds of disease-causing genes should become known. And methods may be developed to identify the presence of these genes with a simple test, so that any doctor could identify them with equipment available in his or her office merely by extracting a quantity of the patient's blood—or any other fluid or tissue containing DNA.

Furthermore, scientists are learning a great deal more about the information contained in our genes. Within the next century, it may become possible to identify much more than just defective genes. It may be possible to determine a person's physical appearance and even certain aspects of their personality from the information contained in their DNA. (As we saw earlier, the environment in which a person grows up is the primary factor determining personality, but it is still possible that predisposition to certain personality types is inherited through the genes.) The more we learn about the genes and the more scientists develop technology for reading genetic information, the more it will be possible to learn from a single sample of an individual's DNA.

And that brings us back to the idea of a government-maintained repository of DNA samples for genetic fingerprinting. Although these samples may be taken solely with DNA fingerprinting in mind, there is always the possibility that they could be used to obtain additional information.

What if an unscrupulous government official decided to eliminate all carriers of a genetic disease from the population? He or she could analyze the genetic data in the DNA repository to determine who carried the gene, then have those individuals sterilized without their consent. Although this is an unlikely scenario in the current political climate, it is impossible to say that it couldn't happen a few decades into the future. Even identifying the presence of a genetic disease in a DNA sample and informing the bearer that he or she possessed it would constitute an unwarranted invasion of privacy. And insurance companies might pay large amounts of money to obtain such information, then refuse to write policies for those at risk of early death or crippling illness.

Even at present, it might be possible to use such samples to identify the carriers of a condition such as AIDS, not by analyzing the genetic information but by testing the fluid in which the sample is contained. Blood from which DNA samples were extracted could be used to test for the AIDS virus, for instance. And the information derived from that test could be used in any number of ways to harm the persons who donated the samples. They could be fired from their jobs, ostracized by their friends, even denied medical benefits.

We can hope that this scenario turns out to be as farfetched as it sounds. But the FBI and other organizations are already urging that libraries of genetic information be compiled for DNA fingerprinting. It's important that such issues of invasion of privacy be resolved now, before it's too late to stop the advance of this particular technology.

Even so, the most pressing issue growing out of DNA fingerprinting technology remains that of accuracy. As sociologist Gary Marx has put it, observing the field from his position at the Massachusetts Institute of Technology, "One [risk] is that the [DNA] technologies work and the other is that they don't."[1] At the one extreme—if they work—they might provide too much information and become an invasion of privacy. At the other extreme—if they don't work —innocent people might suffer.

It's important, then, that we have some idea of just how effective DNA fingerprinting technology is. In the last chapter, we looked at the debate between the forensic scientists on one side and certain biologists and geneticists on the other side, but the issue was unresolved. Is there any hope that it will be resolved in the near future?

There may be. Although the Ohio trial mentioned in the last chapter had not yet come to an end at this writing, a ruling has been made by a magistrate associated with the trial as to the admissibility of evidence derived through genetic fingerprinting tech-

[1] J. Markoff, "A New Breed of Snoopier Computers," *The New York Times*, June 5, 1988 (Sect. 4).

niques. While it's doubtful that this ruling will resolve the debate between scientists over the precise accuracy of the technology, at least it provides a legal precedent that should govern the forensic use of DNA fingerprinting in the near future.

The magistrate, James E. Carr of the Federal District Court in Toledo, Ohio, ruled that DNA fingerprinting evidence *is* admissible in criminal trials. Interestingly, at the same time he disparaged the quality of the DNA evidence presented by the FBI in this particular case, referring to the "remarkably poor quality of the FBI's work and infidelity to important scientific principles."[2] But he nonetheless ruled that the tests could be used in the trial.

In the course of making the decision, Magistrate Carr heard arguments from scientists on both sides of the issue. He admitted that much of the argument about the potential inaccuracy of the DNA evidence was valid. Yet this did not disqualify the evidence from being used in trials, Carr said. It is only necessary that juries be informed of the possible inaccuracy of the results. It is then up to the jury to decide whether the evidence is persuasive or not. Furthermore, he ruled that it was not necessary to have any kind of scientific consensus about the validity of DNA testing before it could be used forensically.

Not surprisingly, opponents of DNA fingerprinting technology were infuriated by this ruling. Peter Neufeld, who is involved in the case as a defense lawyer, said, "I think [Carr] is wrong on the law. True, you don't need unanimity [of scientists], but you do need consensus."[3] In other words, there will

---

[2] Katherine Bishop, "A Victory for Genetic Fingerprinting," *The New York Times,* November 16, 1990, page 137.
[3] *Ibid.*

always be scientists who will dissent from a generally accepted scientific theory or philosophy, but there should at least be some kind of general agreement among scientists before a technology is used in such a serious arena as a court of law.

His colleague and fellow defense lawyer Barry Scheck added, "There's no dispute that there is no need for unanimity, but the law in California, New York and most Federal circuits is that you need consensus—that is, a substantial majority."

Despite these objections to Carr's decision, his ruling bodes well for the future of DNA fingerprinting in forensics. This does not mean that there is no room in the future for the techniques to be improved, however. To the contrary, it is now more important than ever that standardized genetic fingerprinting techniques be established and that DNA tests be performed in laboratories under carefully controlled conditions to assure that the evidence used in trials such as those described in this book be of the highest possible standards.

Until that happens, however, we can expect to see repeated courtroom battles between scientists hired by the prosecution and scientists hired by the defense over the specific quality of the DNA evidence presented in each and every case.

Whatever the future of DNA fingerprinting in criminal trials, there are still other arenas in which it will remain a valuable technique for a long time to come. We saw in Chapter Three, for instance, that DNA analysis provides an ideal method of resolving paternity suits. However, that is only one of the many other uses that scientists have been finding for DNA fingerprinting. We'll look at some of the others in the next chapter.

SEVEN
OTHER APPLICATIONS

The "dirty war" lasted for seven years. From 1976 to 1983, the military regime that ruled Argentina enforced its supremacy with an iron hand. Anyone who opposed the government disappeared mysteriously in the night, never to be seen again. By the time the military government stepped down, more than 12,000 dissidents—perhaps as many as 20,000—had vanished and were apparently dead.

Children had vanished, too. In some cases they had been kidnapped along with their parents; in other cases, pregnant mothers captured by the government had been allowed to give birth before they died. The children were not killed, however; instead, they were sold or given away to friends of the government. A black market in babies thrived in Argentina during the years of the dirty war.

Raul Alfonsin, the head of the government that succeeded the military regime, vowed to locate the children who had disappeared during those seven dark years. But most of the children had been too young when they vanished to remember anything about their previous lives; some had never known another life. Locating these children looked to be a daunting task.

A group known as the Abuelas dela Plaza de Mayo (Spanish for the Grandmothers of the Plaza of May) vowed to locate the missing children, many of whom were their grandchildren, and restore them to their rightful homes. They turned for help to the American Association for the Advancement of Science (AAAS) in the United States. Would it be possible, they wanted to know, to perform some sort of paternity testing on children who were believed to have been kidnapped during the dirty war? Could the children be identified and returned to their rightful grandparents?

Yes, they were told. A team of geneticists, headed by Mary-Claire King, was sent to Argentina to perform bloodtesting on children believed to have been kidnapped during the war. The technique that the team used initially to identify the parentage (and grandparentage) of these children was not DNA fingerprinting (which had not been invented yet) but a similar methodology. Blood was taken from the children and the blood cells were examined for certain antigens, known as human leukocyte antigens (HLA), which are inherited within families. Blood was then taken from all of those believed to be relatives of the child (which usually meant the grandparents, the parents themselves having been killed in the dirty war) and the antigens were compared.

If the antigens on the child's blood cells proved to be a combination of the antigens found on the grandparents' cells, the child must almost certainly be a descendant of those grandparents. (King estimated that the technique had about 1 chance in 500 of being mistaken.)

However, this technique required that authorities in Argentina already have some idea who the grandparents of the child were. In many cases, the child's family history was completely unknown and hundreds of people had to be tested. And in many cases, not enough potential relatives of the child were available to make the tests complete.

What was needed was a test that only required comparison with one possible relative. Such a test was eventually devised by King and Cristian Orrego of the AAAS. It involved, in effect, performing a kind of DNA fingerprinting on *mitochondrial DNA.*

Mitochondria are tiny organelles that swim about in the fluid of the human cell (as well as the cells of most other living creatures on this planet). They are diminutive powerhouses that supply most of the energy in every cell. Many biologists believe that mitochondria were once a separate species, until they came to live in cooperative symbiosis with our distant one-celled ancestors more than a billion years ago. Although no mitochondria are found outside the cells of plants and animals, they still possess their own genes and their own genetic code. When cells split in two to produce new cells, the mitochondria reproduce on their own, with a certain number of mitochondria ending up in each of the resulting cells.

When a baby is conceived, it receives its genes from both the mother and the father, but it receives its mitochondria only from the mother. Thus, the mitochondrial DNA is passed down virtually unchanged from generation to generation, from mother to son and mother to daughter.

If the DNA fingerprint of an individual's mitochondrial DNA is compared with the DNA fingerprint of that individual's mother's mitochondrial DNA, it should be virtually identical. On the other hand, it will not be identical at all when compared with the father's DNA. Thus, mitochondrial DNA provides an excellent means of identifying the mother and grandmother of a child, but an unreliable means of identifying the father and grandfather.

The most attractive thing about mitochondrial DNA, however, is that it remains relatively unchanged from one generation to the next (though over many generations changes do occur). Ordinary DNA, on the other hand, changes dramatically from generation to generation because of the way the father's genes are intermingled with the mother's. When identifying children through mitochondrial DNA fingerprints, it is not necessary to take fingerprints from a large number of family members in order to examine all possible gene combinations that the child may have inherited; one is quite enough.

As of mid-1990, forty-eight of the children of the "disappeareds" had been returned to their families. Alas, as many as 200 children may still remain unidentified. As time passes, these children will grow older, and eventually it may be too late to return them to their families. They will be adults with lives of their own.

DNA fingerprinting (as well as other forensic techniques) is also becoming a common technique for catching poachers—hunters who kill legally protected animals. The problem is not so much one of identifying who the poachers are as of identifying that poaching has taken place at all.

The U.S. Fish and Wildlife Service has set-up a laboratory in Ashland, Oregon, to identify clues to poaching activity. In order to identify that poaching has taken place, it is necessary to show that a dead animal (or, more often, a byproduct created from that animal's body) was in fact the protected animal that authorities suspect it to be.

For instance, it is legal to hunt and kill certain animals in certain areas but illegal in others. But if the poacher kills the animal in an area where it is illegal to do so, then moves the carcass to an area where it is legal (or into his or her home), it is difficult to prove that the animal was killed in the wrong place.

Enter DNA fingerprinting. Because animals tend to breed within a limited geographic range (thus exchanging their genes only with other animals in that area), it is possible to show that there are distinct differences in the DNA fingerprints of an animal born and bred in one area and an animal born and bred in another.

To this end, Stephen Fain of the U.S. Wildlife Service is amassing a collection of tissue samples from elk and bear. He says that he can already tell the difference between DNA taken from the tissue of an Alaskan bear and DNA taken from the tissue of a California bear. And he is developing techniques for performing DNA fingerprinting on tanned leather, so that even garments can be identified as having been made from the bodies of protected species.

One of the major poaching problems worldwide is the trade in ivory taken from the tusks of African elephants. At present, the ivory trade is banned in a number of African countries, but soon the ban may be lifted in three of these countries: Botswana, South Africa, and Zimbabwe. The crucial question facing African authorities—and authorities in countries to which the ivory is likely to be exported—is how to tell the difference between ivory from elephants in these three countries and ivory found elsewhere.

Although it's impossible to perform DNA fingerprinting on an elephant's tusk, poachers (as well as legitimate ivory hunters) often leave pieces of elephant meat attached to the tusks that they sell. Wildlife biologist Nick Georgiadis has begun sending samples of such tissues to John C. Patton, a DNA

identification expert at Washington University in St. Louis, Missouri. Just as Stephen Fain studies the DNA of bears in North America, Patton is currently studying the DNA of African elephants to see if he can identify regional differences that could lead to accurate identification methods. If he can, then it should be possible to selectively enforce bans on the ivory trade; if he can't, then poachers will simply be able to take ivory poached in countries where the trade is banned to countries where it is not, and claim that it was taken legally.

Many of the animals being poached in the United States, Africa, and elsewhere are endangered species. Even without the threat of poaching, many of these species may disappear from the face of the earth in the near future. Putting an end to poaching may give these species a second chance at survival, but DNA fingerprinting can help endangered species in other ways as well.

The continued existence of the whooping crane has been in doubt for most of this century. In 1938, there were only eighteen of these North American birds left on earth. Now there are 135. Though their numbers are improving, the whooping crane is not yet out of danger.

To help the whoopers (as they are known) to survive, wildlife ecologists will sometimes take the

DNA profiling could be of use in catching elephant poachers. It would enable investigators to distinguish between tusks originating from countries where the ivory trade is prohibited and those from countries where it is permitted.

birds into captivity to give them a chance to breed, then return any offspring to the wild to be reared by other birds. But when performing this sort of captive breeding, it is important not to breed two birds who have a close genetic relationship. Otherwise, undesirable genes are likely to reinforce each other, making the resulting offspring sickly and unprepared to survive. The ideal mating should take place between completely unrelated birds.

But how can you tell if two birds are related? The birds themselves may know, but to human beings the family resemblances between individual birds are not easy to see.

DNA fingerprinting to the rescue! Just as DNA fingerprints can be used to show if two individuals are closely related, they can also be used to show that two individuals (be they human or bird) are *not* closely related. Jonathan Longmire of the Los Alamos National Laboratory is applying DNA fingerprinting techniques to a flock of birds currently being kept at a wildlife center in Maryland, to provide guidelines for captive breeding among those birds.

Much the same thing is being done with the California condor, perhaps the rarest bird of all. Only twenty-seven California condors are known to exist at present, and all of them are in captivity. The birds are being carefully bred, but there are so few of

The whooping crane, an endangered species. When breeding whooping cranes in captivity, it is undesirable to mate two birds with a close genetic relationship. DNA fingerprinting can be used to select compatible mates.

them that it is difficult to find two birds sufficiently distant genetically to mate successfully. DNA fingerprinting could be used to determine which birds have the most genes in common (and therefore should not be mated) and which have the least genes in common (and therefore should be mated).

Perhaps one of the oddest uses of DNA fingerprinting is in evolutionary biology, the study of the ways in which living organisms change over time. Because these changes obviously involve genes, there would seem to be an obvious place for DNA fingerprinting in these studies. But the area where evolutionary scientists are using DNA fingerprinting is an unexpected one: they are using it to see if animals are raising their own children or the children of some other animal.

One of the thorniest areas of evolutionary study is the study of altruism. Altruistic behavior is defined as behavior by an animal that reduces that animal's chances of survival (however slightly) while increasing another animal's chance of surviving.

We have all seen examples of altruism in human beings, from the truly heroic behavior of individuals who risk (and even sacrifice) their lives to save another person, to the quiet generosity of people who give away some of their own money to help others. Altruistic behavior can also be observed in the animal world, occasionally to the surprise of scientists.

Why shouldn't animals behave altruistically? Unlike human beings, who have the intelligence to decide whether or not they wish to act altruistically, most animal behavior is instinctual, or largely so. Animals are born with certain innate behavior patterns, or *instincts,* and these patterns are often determined by their genes. This is why animals don't have to go to school to learn how to survive within their habitats; they are born with the knowledge they need or with the tools needed to gain that knowledge rapidly. Thus, animal behavior is at least in part genetic, determined by evolution.

If animals behave altruistically, then, it is probably because they have genes that code for altruistic behavior. But where did these genes come from? According to evolutionary biologists, genes develop first by accidental mutation (errors in copying genes from one generation to the next), but they last because they help the animal who inherits them to survive better than related animals who don't have that particular gene. But a gene for altruism would actually *lower* an animal's chance of survival. A gene for altruism would therefore be self-destructive and would not survive for many generations before it was eliminated altogether from the population.

Yet altruistic behavior *is* observed in the animal world and therefore genes for that altruistic behavior must exist. Prairie dogs, for instance, will cry out when they see a predator attacking a prairie dog hill, giving the other prairie dogs in the hill advance warning of the predator's approach. But the prairie dog who cries out draws the attention of the predator to itself, thus lowering its own chance of survival.

Why do altruistic genes evolve? The answer, say evolutionary biologists, is something called *kin selection*. Although the prairie dog in the previous example is risking his own genes by crying out a warning at the approach of a predator, he is helping to assure the survival of his relatives in the prairie dog hill, many of whom carry the same gene! Thus, the gene is assuring its *own* survival (or the survival of the many copies of itself in the prairie dog hill), but not necessarily the survival of the individual prairie dog.

Kin selection is still largely theoretical. To verify

that it actually works, it is necessary for scientists to watch the behavior of animals in the wild and see if altruistic behavior actually does enhance the success of an animal's genes. One place where this sort of behavior can be observed is in the nests of birds.

Certain species of birds are known to place their eggs in the nests of other birds when the other birds aren't looking, in order to trick the other bird into raising their young for them. This gives the trickster bird the opportunity to have more children than otherwise, because the burden of raising their earlier children is no longer on their shoulders but on the shoulders of the other birds. And this in turn allows them to create more copies of their own genes, which increases their evolutionary fitness.

A bird who raises an egg placed in its nest by the trickster bird could be said to be engaging in altruistic behavior, since raising a bird that does not carry its genes does not help it to pass its genes on to another generation. Scientists study such birds to see how many of the young birds that they raise are their own offspring and how many are the offspring of other birds.

Unfortunately, it is often impossible to tell. If the trickster is not actually observed placing the egg in the nest, it isn't easy to determine which eggs belong to the birds in the nest and which do not. But DNA fingerprinting of the chicks can resolve the dilemma. If the DNA of the young birds does not match the DNA of the birds who raised them, then the birds have indeed been engaging in altruistic behavior. If the DNA does match, then they have not.

Nicholas Davies, a biologist at Cambridge University in England, has used DNA fingerprinting in a particularly elaborate study of hedge sparrows at the university's botanical gardens. These birds engage in mating behavior that would make the characters on a television soap opera blush. Some are polyandrous (the female bird has more than one mate), some are polygynous (the male bird has more than one mate) and some are polygynandrous (both sexes have more than one mate). Some are even monogamous.

Curious about which of these mating behaviors led to the greatest reproductive success, Davies has used DNA fingerprinting to determine which chicks are the offspring of which male and female birds. The result has revealed some surprises about the birds' mating habits, and a few details that are not so surprising. In a polyandrous relationship, for instance, the female bird has a very high reproductive success, because she has two males helping to raise her children. But the males don't do so well; with only one mate between them, they average only half the children that they could have in a monogamous relationship. On the other hand, they benefit to some extent from the help the other male offers in raising the chicks.

The applications of DNA fingerprinting are many and varied. Almost certainly it will remain a major forensic technique once scientists have had a chance to work out a stronger theoretical basis for the technology, and standards have been applied to the laboratories that perform the work.

Some people have even gone so far as to suggest that one day everyone will have their DNA typed at birth and universal records of DNA types (complete with blood and tissue samples) will be kept at a central repository, so that DNA from the scene of a crime can be instantly matched to provide the identity of the perpetrator. However, others have suggested that such a central DNA data bank would represent an unconstitutional invasion of privacy and would allow other information to be gleaned from individuals' genes than just DNA fingerprints. Whether such a data bank will ever be feasible, either technologically or politically, remains to be seen.

Nonetheless, DNA fingerprinting is here to stay. No matter its future in forensics, DNA fingerprinting will almost certainly continue to be used in paternity testing and in many other applications.

GLOSSARY

Active sites. The locations on the surface of enzymes where molecules are fitted into place long enough to react chemically with other molecules.

Agarose. The substance in which DNA fragments are placed during gel electrophoresis.

Amino acids. The molecules that serve as the building blocks of protein molecules.

Antigen. Tiny structures found on the surface of living cells, including blood cells.

Atoms. Tiny particles that are the basic building blocks of all matter.

Bands. The striped markings on a DNA fingerprint that represent the strips of radioactively tagged DNA fragments in a lane on a gel electrophoresis plate.

Band-shift. A phenomenon in which the DNA fragments in one lane of a gel electrophoresis plate move faster than the fragments in another, causing otherwise identical bands to shift left or right relative to one another.

Bases. The four varieties of nucleotides that make up DNA molecules, including adenosine, guanine, thymine, and cytosine.

Blood-typing. The identification of blood by antigen type.

Chromosomes. Large molecules found in the center of living cells that contain genetic information.

Control bands. Bands on a DNA fingerprint, indicating the position of monomorphic probes and designed to identify the presence of band-shifting.

Criminalistics. The study of physical evidence left at the scene of a crime.

DNA. Short for deoxyribonucleic acid; the substance of which chromosomes are made.

DNA replication. The process by which DNA molecules make copies of themselves.

Electric charge. A property of certain particles that causes them to repel or attract one another; either negative or positive in nature.

Enzymes. Protein molecules that control the chemical reactions taking place within a cell.

Exons. Seemingly meaningless sequences of base pairs on a chromosome, which do not code for proteins.

Fingerprinting. The cataloging and identification of the markings left behind by contact with bare fingertips.

Fissions. The splitting apart of old cells to create new cells.

Forensics. The science of interpreting clues to a crime.

Gel electrophoresis. A process by which scientists can sort pieces of DNA according to size.

Genes. Hereditary units passed from generation to generation that determine the physical makeup of the organism receiving them.

Introns. The sequences of base pairs on a chromosome, which code for protein molecules.

Kin selection. An evolutionary process by which an individual organism is motivated to protect those bearing the same genes.

Lanes. The divisions on the surface of a gel electrophoresis plate in which DNA samples are placed.

Markers. Gene sequences in known positions on a chromosome used to identify the presence of nearby sequences of unknown position.

Mitochondrial DNA. The chromosomes of the mitochondria, organelles found within the cells of higher organisms. Mitochondria are believed to have once been separate organisms themselves.

Molecules. Chains of atoms.

Monomorphic probes. Identical DNA fragments added to the lanes of a gel electrophoresis plate to identify, and compensate for, the presence of band-shifting.

Negative charge. One of two varieties of electric charge *(see* Positive charge).

Nucleotides. The molecules that are the building blocks of DNA molecules.

Nucleus. The structure in the center of many living cells in which the chromosomes are found.

Oligonucleotide primers. Fragments of DNA designed to attach themselves to a larger fragment of DNA at the ends of a sequence to be cloned via the polymerase chain reaction (PCR).

Papillary ridges. Tiny lines of flesh at the tips of the fingers, which create fingerprint patterns.

Pattern area. The central portion of a fingerprint.

Polymerase chain reaction (PCR). A process by which multiple copies of a specific DNA fragment can be cloned quickly and inexpensively.

Positive charge. One of two varieties of electric charge.

Protein molecules. Large chains of atoms made up of smaller molecules called amino acids.

Radioactive probes. Radioactively labeled molecules designed to attach themselves to specific sequences of base pairs.

Recessive gene. A "quiet" gene that can be passed on for many generations without being expressed.

Recombinant DNA. The body of techniques used by biologists to combine fragments of genes from two or more organisms in a single organism (usually a bacterium).

Restriction enzyme. An enzyme that can slice DNA molecules into several fragments; used by biologists to recombine genes into new sequences.

FOR FURTHER READING

Baskin, Yvonne, "DNA Unlimited," *Discover,* July 1990, pp. 76–79.

Beardsley, Tim, "For the Birds," *Scientific American,* June 1988, p. 32.

———"Fowl Play," *Scientific American,* October 1990, p. 28.

Bishop, Katherine, "A Victory for Genetic Fingerprinting," *The New York Times,* November 16, 1990.

Cherfas, Jeremy, "Science Gives Ivory a Sense of Identity," *Science,* December 1, 1989, pp. 1120–1121.

Johnson, Kirk, "DNA 'Fingerprinting' Tests Becoming a Factor in Courts," *The New York Times,* February 7, 1988.

Kolata, Gina, "Some Scientists Doubt the Value of 'Genetic Fingerprint' Evidence," *The New York Times,* January 29, 1990.

Labaton, Stephen, "DNA Fingerprinting Showdown Expected in Ohio," *The New York Times,* June 22, 1990.

Lewin, Roger, "DNA Typing Is Called Flawed," *Science,* July 28, 1989, p. 355.

———"DNA Typing on the Witness Stand," *Science,* June 2, 1989, pp. 1033–1035.

———"Judging Paternity in the Hedge Sparrow's World," *Science,* March 31, 1989, pp. 1663–1664.

———"Limits to DNA Fingerprinting," *Science,* March 24, 1988, pp. 1549–1551.

Lewis, Rick, "DNA Fingerprinting: Witness for the Prosecution," *Discover,* June 1988, pp. 44–52.

Markoff, John, "A New Breed of Snoopier Computers," *The New York Times,* June 5, 1988.

Michaud, Stephen, "DNA Detectives," *The New York Times Magazine,* December 6, 1988, pp. 70–73.

Neufeld, Peter J., and Neville Colman, "When Science Takes the Witness Stand," *Scientific American,* May 1990, pp. 46–53.

Noonan, David, "Genes of War," *Discover,* October 1990, pp. 46–52.

Norman, Colin, "Caution Urged on DNA Fingerprinting," *Science,* August 18, 1989, p. 699.

———"Maine Case Deals Blow to DNA Fingerprinting," *Science,* December 22, 1989, pp. 1556–1558.

Toufexis, Anastasia, "Convicted by their Genes," *Time,* October 31, 1988, p. 74.

Vogel, Shawna, "The Case of the Unraveling DNA," *Discover,* January 1990, pp. 46–47.

Wambaugh, Joseph, *The Blooding,* Bantam Books, New York, 1989.

Wilkerson, Isabel, "Tests May End 10-Year Rape Dispute," *The New York Times,* February 7, 1988.

INDEX

Blood tests, 15–16, 43
Blood-typing, 15–16, 43
Bureau of Criminal
  Identification,
  International
  Association of Chiefs
  of Police,
  13–14

California condor, 95–96
Cambridge University,
  England, 98
Cancer, 81
Carr, James E., 84, 85
Castro, José, 65–66, 69
Cellmark, 49, 67, 68, 72
Cells, 21–23, 27, 89
Central pocket loop
  fingerprint, 13
Cetus Corporation, 47
Chromosomes, 17, 21–27,
  31–33, 48, 79, 80
Cold Spring Harbor
  Laboratory, New
  York, 68
Constitution of the
  United States, 75–76
Control bands, 65
Criminalistics, 10–11
Cytosine (C), 23–25

Davies, Nicholas, 98–99
DNA (deoxyribonucleic
  acid), 23–27, 32, 48
  (see also DNA
  fingerprinting)

DNA fingerprinting
  accuracy of, 75
  in Argentina, 89–90
  California condor
    and, 95–96
  error in, 41, 76–77
  in evolutionary
    biology, 96–99
  for immigration
    purposes, 43–47
  judges and, 57, 61,
    70, 84–85
  libraries for, 77–83,
    99–100
  in Mann-Ashworth
    murder cases, 54–
    58
  in Ohio murder
    case, 72, 83–84
  in Orlando rape
    cases, 59–61
  in paternity cases,
    41–43, 45, 47, 85,
    100
  poacher catching
    and, 90–93
  in Ponce murder
    case, 65–70
  problems with, 63–
    73
  process of, 33–41
  promise of, 16
  for solving crimes,
    41, 45, 47, 49, 54–
    61, 83–85, 100
  whooping cranes
    and, 94, 95

ABOUT THE AUTHOR

Christopher Lampton has written over thirty books on such diverse science subjects as astronomy, computers, ecology, and dinosaurs. His recent books for Franklin Watts include *Gene Technology* and *Telecommunications: From Telegraphs to Modems.* In addition to his nonfiction, Mr. Lampton has written four science fiction novels. He has a degree in broadcast journalism and makes his home in Silver Spring, Maryland.